From Emoji to Empathy

Mastering Customer Service in the Digital Era

Susan Williamson

only. All effort has been executed to present accurate, up to date, reliable, complete information. No warranties of any kind are declared or implied. Readers acknowledge that the author is not engaged in the rendering of legal, financial, medical or professional advice. The content within this book has been derived from various sources. Please consult a licensed professional before attempting any techniques outlined in this book.

By reading this document, the reader agrees that under no circumstances is the author responsible for any losses, direct or indirect, that are incurred as a result of the use of the information contained within this document, including, but not limited to, errors, omissions, or inaccuracies.

Table of Contents

Introduction

Have you ever left a store or ended a call feeling genuinely uplifted, not just because of what you purchased, but also because of the warmth and understanding of the service you received? A time when every interaction leaves you with that glowing impression can be a reality—a world where excellent service is the norm, not the exception. This is the vision we're setting out to achieve within these pages. It's about reimagining customer service for today's fast-paced, overwhelming-with-choices environment, where businesses either thrive through their service excellence or dwindle under the weight of indifference.

We are entering what can be termed the golden age of customer service, and the stakes have never been higher. With countless options available at one's fingertips, it's no longer enough to offer just a good product or a fair price. Customers are seeking experiences—they crave connections that emphasize human interaction. It's in these connections that companies build their brand's reputation and foster true loyalty. To back this statement, let me tell you about recent studies that are evidence of an eye-opening reality: a staggering 70% of customers are willing to pay more for an elevated service experience. The kind of service that doesn't just end with a transaction but starts a relationship.

Yet, behind each cheerful front-line service representative lies a host of challenges that are far from trivial. Customer service managers and teams often find themselves juggling high expectations against the backdrop of limited resources. From managing long queues and handling irate callers to adapting to rapidly evolving technologies, the hurdles can sometimes feel insurmountable. Add to this the emotional strain of maneuvering difficult interactions, and it's clear why service roles are among the most demanding. But therein lies the opportunity; these challenges demand innovation in service delivery and hold the potential for tremendous growth, both personally and professionally.

Enter *From Emoji to Empathy: Mastering Customer Service in the Digital Era*, designed to be your compass in navigating the complex landscape of modern customer service. This book is not just about addressing the struggles faced daily by teams and managers; and it's about transforming these struggles into stepping stones toward better service delivery. Here, you'll discover practical frameworks infused with emotional intelligence because understanding the heart of your customer is just as important as solving their concerns. You'll learn how to harness technology without losing the human touch, maintain team motivation even during challenging times, and create systems that streamline processes while enriching personal interactions.

Who Is Behind These Words?

My journey in customer service spans over two decades, beginning in the 1990s at Kmart and evolving into a role as a corporate flight attendant on private jets. I'm now retired, but until recently, I provided elite service to CEOs, board members, and high-profile clients. Throughout my career, I've held roles ranging from frontline support to team leadership. My many positions have taught me invaluable insights into what it takes to build genuine connections with customers and foster loyalty in today's seemingly detached world.

I've seen firsthand how service can make or break a customer's experience. I've also witnessed a troubling trend: the decline of empathy and patience in service roles. Employees rolling their eyes, lacking patience, and failing to smile have become all too common. This inspired me to write this book—a guide to help build a better future for customer service, where AI, instant communication, and sky-high expectations are reshaping the landscape.

Through this book, I promise you three things: humor, honesty, and practical tips. My goal is to speak to you directly, sharing stories, insights, and real-world examples that make sense, inspire, and are readily applicable to your unique setting—whether you manage a bustling team or run a small enterprise. You'll encounter actionable solutions tailored to refine current practices and revolutionize how your service is perceived by those who matter most: your customers.

Our journey together will shed light on how to:

- **Empower your team** with tools and strategies that boost service effectiveness and deepen customer engagement.
- **Promote emotional intelligence** in every interaction, fostering stronger connections and lasting loyalty.
- **Measure and improve customer satisfaction** through actionable insights and continuous improvement practices.

To my audience of customer service managers and their teams: Consider this book your toolkit, offering new ways to elevate your team's performance while enriching everyday service experiences. Perhaps you're rethinking your entire approach or simply looking to sharpen your current skills, either way, there's something here for everyone focused on making a noticeable impact.

For entrepreneurs and small business owners: Herein lies the insight required to embed exceptional service seamlessly into the DNA of your business operations. As you seek to improve service experiences, use the lessons within to set the stage for exceptional customer journeys that don't just satisfy but delight.

So, welcome to this transformational process. By choosing to embrace the concepts outlined in these chapters, you're committing to a path where every customer interaction counts, where service becomes synonymous with success, and where your efforts to keep customers coming back again and again. Let's set sail on this adventure toward crafting unforgettable service experiences that not only meet but exceed the escalating expectations in today's dynamic marketplace. Together, we'll ensure that your service stands out, leaving a legacy of satisfaction and loyalty that echoes beyond a single purchase.

Chapter 1: Understanding Customer Service Excellence

In today's world, where customers have more choices than ever, great service isn't just a nice touch—it's the secret weapon that keeps them coming back. Sure, competitive prices and flashy products might get people through the digital or actual door, but it's the experience they remember. The way a business makes them feel is what turns a onetime buyer into a lifelong customer.

Exceptional service isn't just about solving problems, either; it's about creating moments—those small but powerful interactions that build trust, loyalty, and even brand advocacy. A seamless return process, a genuinely helpful conversation, or a personal touch that makes someone feel valued—these things stick with people. And when done right, they lead to repeat business, glowing reviews, and long-term success.

So, what does it take to deliver truly outstanding service? That's exactly what we're diving into in this chapter. We'll break down the key ingredients of great service, explore how they impact business growth, and tackle the real-world challenges teams face every day.

Whether you're leading a customer service team, running your own business, or simply looking to up your game, this chapter will give you the insights and strategies you need to create meaningful, lasting connections with your customers.

The Importance of Customer Service in Business Success

Think about the last time you had an amazing customer service experience—the kind that made you want to tell everyone about it. Maybe it was the barista who remembered your order and your dog's name or the tech support rep who actually made fixing your issue feel effortless. That kind of service becomes a game-changer for businesses. In a world where customers have endless options, products and prices alone won't cut it. What really sets a business apart is how it makes people feel.

Great service builds trust. When customers feel valued, heard, and understood, they're far more likely to come back. And that's huge because keeping an existing customer reduces costs significantly compared to finding a new one. Businesses that focus on customer service see higher retention rates, more referrals, and a steady stream of revenue that doesn't rely on throwing piles of cash into advertising (Dwivedi et al., 2024).

So, what exactly is a repeat customer, and why does repeat business matter so much? A repeat customer is someone who doesn't just buy from you once; they keep coming back. The more they return, the more profitable they become. Loyal customers spend more over time, require less convincing to make a purchase, and are more likely to recommend your business to others. Plus, having a strong base of repeat customers makes revenue more predictable and sustainable, reducing the pressure to constantly chase new leads. Repeat business also minimizes the need for costly marketing efforts, allowing companies to allocate resources more efficiently.

Beyond just bringing in sales, great service builds a brand's reputation. Happy customers talk. They tell friends, leave glowing reviews, and turn into your best (and free!) marketing team. On the flip side, bad experiences spread like wildfire through word of mouth and social media—one negative interaction can lead to scathing reviews and a reputation hit that's tough to recover from (Suley and Yuanqiong, 2019).

And if you need a hard number to back this up, here's the deal: companies that prioritize customer satisfaction consistently outperform their competitors in revenue and market share. Research shows a direct link between exceptional service and profitability—businesses that invest in customer experience often see stronger sales, higher retention rates, and better brand positioning. It's not just about "being nice" to customers; it's a proven strategy for long-term success. Performance metrics, such as Net Promoter Scores (NPS) and customer satisfaction ratings, provide tangible proof that great service translates to better financial results.

In short, every single customer interaction is an opportunity. Do it right, and you're not just making a sale—you're strengthening trust, increasing customer lifetime value, and creating a fan for life. On the flip side, a poor experience can send customers straight to a competitor, sometimes for good. The stakes are high, but the rewards of getting customer service right are even higher.

Key Components of Excellent Customer Service

Great customer service can be described as a box that businesses check off, but it must be an experience that customers remember for a long time. It's like crafting the perfect dish: the right mix of ingredients turns something ordinary into something unforgettable. The key elements of exceptional service: personalization, responsiveness, consistency, and empowerment—work together to create customer interactions that leave a lasting impact.

- **Personalization:** At the core of great service is personalization—the ability to make customers feel like more than just a transaction. It's that feeling you get when the barista knows your order before you say a word or when a customer support agent remembers your last conversation. These small touches build emotional connections and inspire loyalty. Businesses can use customer data (ethically, of course) to anticipate needs, customize recommendations, and show genuine appreciation. Studies have shown that when companies tailor their service, customers are more likely to return and spend more over time (Heath, 2019).

- **Responsiveness:** Then there's responsiveness—because in today's fast-moving world, nobody likes waiting. Whether it's answering a question, resolving an issue, or simply acknowledging a request, speed matters, customers want to know they're a priority, and quick, thoughtful responses make all the difference. A proactive approach, like reaching out before a problem is noticed through feedback and analytics escalates, can turn a potential frustration into a moment of trust (Reji, 2023). Imagine a software company noticing a common issue in user forums and releasing an update before customers even complain—this kind of forward-thinking service builds long-term credibility.

- **Consistency:** This point is another non-negotiable. Customers interact with businesses across multiple channels—social media, phone calls, in-store visits—and they expect the same level of service no matter where they go. A brand that delivers friendly, efficient support online but drops the ball in-store creates confusion and erodes trust. When businesses ensure uniform service across all touchpoints, they build reliability and strengthen their brand image (Heath, 2019).

- **Employee empowerment:** Empowerment is the secret ingredient that takes service from good to great. When frontline employees have the authority to solve problems on the spot, resolutions are faster, and customers walk away happier. It's frustrating when a simple issue requires multiple approvals, leading to unnecessary delays. Instead, giving employees clear guidelines on how much autonomy they have—whether it's offering discounts, replacing products, or waiving fees—allows them to act quickly and effectively. A hotel chain that lets front desk staff offer complimentary upgrades during booking mishaps, for example, can turn a potential frustration into a positive memory. Plus, empowered employees feel more confident and engaged, which translates into better service across the board.

Mastering these components makes customers happy at the moment, but more importantly, it builds relationships that keep them coming back. When businesses personalize interactions, respond quickly, stay consistent, and give employees the tools to succeed, they create a service experience that stands out in any industry.

Common Challenges in Customer Service Roles

As we have widely discussed above, customer service is all about creating positive experiences, but let's be real—it's not always smooth sailing. From handling sky-high customer expectations to dealing with resource constraints, emotional strain, and ever-evolving technology, service teams face plenty of challenges. The key to overcoming these obstacles lies in preparation, adaptability, and a strong support system.

- **Managing high customer expectations:** Customers expect fast, personalized, and flawless service—and meeting those expectations can be tough. Whether it's a seasoned professional or a new hire, the pressure to deliver can feel overwhelming. That's where training comes in. Ongoing development programs help employees stay ahead of customer demands by sharpening their skills and problem-solving abilities. The best training doesn't just cover the basics; it prepares teams to go above and beyond. Regularly reassessing training needs keeps service teams in sync with shifting customer trends, ensuring a culture of continuous learning and improvement (Trinet, 2023).

- **Resource constraints:** Limited staff, tight budgets, and increasing service demands can make maintaining high-quality service feel like an uphill battle. The answer isn't always "hire more people"—it's about working smarter. Businesses can streamline workflows, use automation tools, and optimize team communication to improve efficiency without stretching resources too thin (Gjellebæk et al., 2020). For instance, integrating AI-powered chatbots for routine inquiries allows human agents to focus on more complex issues. Finding innovative ways to do more with less keeps service standards high, even under financial or staffing limitations.

- **Emotional strain on employees:** Dealing with frustrated customers, handling complaints, and maintaining a friendly demeanor all day can take an emotional toll. If stress and burnout aren't addressed, job satisfaction—and ultimately service quality—can suffer. Companies that prioritize employee well-being see better retention and higher engagement. Wellness programs, mental health support, work-life balance, and fostering an open culture where employees feel heard can make a huge difference. Regular check-ins, peer support systems, and recognition programs also help build resilience and prevent burnout (Trinet, 2023).

- **Keeping up with technology:** Technology is a double-edged sword—it can make customer service more efficient, but it can also be intimidating for employees who aren't tech-savvy. The challenge is making sure employees feel comfortable using new tools when implementing them. Businesses should focus on user-friendly systems, offer step-by-step training, and introduce new tech gradually rather than all at once. Training workshops, interactive demos, and even gamified learning sessions can make the process engaging and stress-free. When employees see technology as a tool that helps them (rather than something that replaces them), they're more likely to embrace it.

How to Overcome These Challenges

- **Set clear expectations with customers:** Transparent communication and proactive service help prevent misunderstandings and build trust.
- **Optimize resources effectively:** Lean management techniques and automation can help businesses do more with fewer resources.
- **Support employees emotionally:** Recognizing hard work, offering mental health resources, and promoting work-life balance can boost morale and retention.
- **Make technology adoption easy:** Training, phased rollouts, and hands-on support help employees gain confidence with new tools.

Customer service comes with its fair share of challenges, but businesses that invest in their teams—through training, support, and smart solutions—set themselves up for long-term success. The key is balancing efficiency with empathy, ensuring both customers and employees have the tools they need to thrive.

Conclusion

Delivering outstanding customer experiences takes dedication, but the payoff is huge—stronger relationships, deeper trust, and a brand that truly stands out. This chapter has broken down the key ingredients of great service: personalization, responsiveness, consistency, and empowering employees to make a difference. When businesses focus on these elements, everyday interactions turn into meaningful moments that customers remember.

Companies that commit to these principles don't just meet expectations; they exceed them. Whether they are managers, teams, entrepreneurs, or business owners, applying these principles will deliver great service. Great service builds loyalty, sparks advocacy, and strengthens a brand's reputation. When both employees and customers feel valued, success follows naturally.

Next, we're exploring the role of emotional intelligence in customer service—an essential skill that helps service professionals connect with customers on a deeper level. Understanding emotions, practicing empathy, and responding with care can transform interactions and create experiences that truly resonate.

Chapter 2: The Role of Emotional Intelligence

Have you ever encountered a customer service representative who seemed to truly “get” you? Someone who not only solved your problem but also made you feel heard and valued? That’s the power of emotional intelligence in action.

Every interaction with a customer involves more than just words; it’s about acknowledging their feelings, picking up on unspoken cues, and responding in a way that makes them feel understood. It’s also about managing your own emotions and understanding and responding to the emotions of others. When service professionals tap into emotional intelligence, they move beyond robotic transactions and create genuine connections that build trust and loyalty.

Hold that example in mind, as in this chapter, we'll learn how emotional intelligence shapes customer service experiences. We’ll explore how it helps in de-escalating conflicts, improving communication, and creating lasting customer relationships. You’ll also get practical strategies for developing empathy, mastering active listening, and recognizing emotional cues—all essential for making customers feel understood.

Whether you're leading a service team, running a business, or just looking to sharpen your skills, these insights will help you handle tough situations with confidence and turn everyday interactions into moments that truly matter.

Understanding Emotional Intelligence in Customer Service

In customer service, emotional intelligence isn't just a buzzword—it's a game-changer. But what does it really mean, and why is it so critical in customer interactions? At its core, emotional intelligence is the ability to recognize, understand, and manage emotions—both your own and those of others. It's about being tuned in, not just to what's being said, but to the emotions driving the conversation.

Let's take this example: you're dealing with a frustrated customer. A representative with strong emotional intelligence doesn't just hear the complaint; they sense the frustration, don't get tangled up in their own reactions, regulate their response, and approach the situation with empathy. This ability to connect on an emotional level can make all the difference in de-escalating conflicts and turning tense moments into opportunities to build trust (Borowski, 2024).

Strong customer relationships are as much about what you say as they are about how you make people feel. When emotional intelligence is at play, interactions shift from routine transactions to meaningful connections. Service professionals who can read emotional cues and adjust their approach accordingly create smoother and more positive experiences.

But there's more; emotional intelligence also boosts problem-solving. When a representative can pick up on the emotions behind a customer's frustration, they're better equipped to offer solutions that go beyond surface-level fixes. Instead of just resolving the immediate issue, they address the root cause, leading to better outcomes, stronger customer satisfaction, and, ultimately, higher customer retention (Poletto, 2023).

Empathy is a key player here. It's what allows service professionals to truly understand a customer's perspective. And when customers feel heard and validated, their overall satisfaction skyrockets. Even when things don't go perfectly—maybe there's a shipping delay or a system glitch—customers are far more likely to be patient and forgiving if they feel that someone genuinely cares about their experience.

This kind of emotional connection isn't just good for customers; it's a win for service teams, too. A workplace that prioritizes emotional intelligence fosters better communication, reduces stress, and improves overall job satisfaction. When teams are equipped to manage high-pressure situations with confidence, burnout decreases, and performance improves. It's a ripple effect; happier employees lead to happier customers, and that's the kind of cycle every business wants.

Emotional intelligence is a strategic advantage, not just a soft skill. And in customer service, where every interaction counts, it's one of the most powerful tools you can have.

Developing Empathy and Active Listening Skills

If there's one skill that separates good customer service from truly exceptional service, it's empathy. Pair that with active listening, and you've got a winning formula for understanding customers on a deeper level. But empathy isn't just about nodding along or saying the right things—it's about genuinely feeling what the customer is going through. When people sense that their emotions are acknowledged and validated, they're more likely to trust your brand and stick around. Even a simple phrase like, "I can see why that would be frustrating," can go a long way in making customers feel heard (Call Center Studio, 2023).

I experienced this firsthand at my first job at K-Mart, working in the jewelry department. One day, a little girl—maybe ten or eleven—walked up to the counter in ragged jeans and a worn-out t-shirt. She hesitated before quietly asking to see a small ring.

As I handed it to her, she explained that her dad had dropped her off to find a Mother's Day gift, but she didn't have much money. She was shy, maybe even nervous, but determined. We looked at different pieces, but her heart was set on that one ring—just out of her budget at thirty dollars.

I couldn't let her leave empty-handed, so when she offered what little she had, I covered the rest. When I placed the ring in a box and handed it to her, her face lit up with pure joy. She clutched the tiny package like it was the most important thing in the world.

I didn't have much money myself back then, but even now, I still think about that little girl and how good it felt to help her give her mom the perfect gift. That moment wasn't about a sale—it was about understanding someone's emotions and making a difference.

Active listening takes this even further by ensuring you don't just hear what the customer is saying—you truly understand them. It's picking up on the emotions behind their words and responding in a way that shows you're engaged. Simple techniques, like summarizing their concerns or asking open-ended questions, can make a world of difference. For example, saying, "So, it sounds like you're having trouble with your product delivery?" not only confirms you're on the same page, but also reassures the customer that their issue is being taken seriously (Pollack,

2024). This approach minimizes misunderstandings and keeps the conversation moving toward a solution.

But here's the thing: communication is much more than just words. In face-to-face interactions, body language plays a huge role in conveying empathy. Eye contact, an occasional nod, and leaning in slightly can all signal that you're fully present. These small gestures create an atmosphere of trust, making customers more comfortable opening up about their concerns.

Of course, developing these skills takes practice. That's where structured training comes in. Role-playing exercises, in which agents step into different customer scenarios, can be a powerful way to build empathy. Practicing how to handle frustrated or anxious customers helps teams respond with patience and understanding in real interactions. Feedback loops also play a crucial role—by analyzing real conversations and offering constructive criticism, teams can fine-tune their approach, ensuring a consistently high level of service.

Service Channels and Their Nuances

Different customer service channels require different approaches, and understanding those nuances is key:

- **Phone support:** Tone is everything. Since there's no body language to rely on, verbal affirmations like "I understand" or "I see" help bridge the gap.

Pausing to let the customer fully express themselves—without interruption—also prevents tension from escalating (Pollack, 2024).

- **Live chat and messaging:** Speed matters, but so does warmth. Thoughtful responses, personalized greetings, and even emojis (when appropriate) can help convey friendliness in a text-based conversation. Asking relevant follow-up questions also reassures customers that their concerns are being taken seriously.

- **Email support:** Because emails lack real-time interaction, clarity, and thoroughness are crucial. Summarizing the customer's issue before responding ensures alignment, while a warm and empathetic tone prevents messages from feeling robotic.

For customer service managers and entrepreneurs looking to strengthen their teams, these strategies are invaluable. A company culture that prioritizes empathy and active listening benefits customers and boosts employee morale. When service professionals feel empowered and supported in handling emotional interactions, they're more likely to find fulfillment in their roles. And when teams are engaged and motivated, businesses see stronger customer relationships, improved retention, and a standout reputation.

Active listening and empathy work better when service professionals make these skills second nature. Encouraging employees to practice focused attention, ask clarifying questions like "Can you tell me more about that?" and minimize distractions during conversations can go a long way. Regular role-playing sessions and constructive feedback further refine these abilities, ensuring that teams continue to grow and improve.

At the end of the day, customers don't just remember the solutions you provide—they remember how you made them feel. And that's what keeps them coming back.

Recognizing Emotional Cues From Customers

Great customer service is about understanding people. Customers communicate how they're feeling in countless ways, sometimes without even realizing it. Whether it's the words they choose, the tone of their voice, or even subtle shifts in body language, these emotional cues offer valuable insight into their experience. The key for customer service professionals? Knowing how to recognize and respond to them effectively.

Picking up on these signals can be tricky, though emotional cues aren't always obvious. A frustrated customer might raise their voice, but sometimes, frustration sounds more like short, clipped responses or a sudden change in tone. Likewise, uncertainty can come through in hesitations, softer speech, or phrases like, "I just don't know what to do." Even in text-based interactions, punctuation, word choice, and phrasing can hint at a customer's emotions. The challenge lies in tuning in and responding in a way that acknowledges their feelings while guiding the conversation toward a solution.

When customer service representatives get this right, the impact is huge. Let's say a customer is upset about a delayed delivery. If a representative picks up on their frustration—not just from their words, but also from their tone—they can acknowledge it before jumping to a solution. A response like, "I completely understand how frustrating delays can be. Let's see what we can do to make this right," shows empathy and shifts the focus toward resolution. Small adjustments like this can make the difference between an angry customer and one who feels valued and heard.

Beyond improving individual interactions, recognizing emotional cues also helps prevent conflicts. When customers feel that their emotions are acknowledged and respected, they're less likely to escalate a situation. Over time, this fosters deeper trust and loyalty, strengthening the relationship between customers and businesses.

Techniques for Identifying Emotional Cues

So, how can customer service professionals sharpen their ability to recognize these signals?

- **Active observation:** The best customer service representatives don't just listen to what's being said—they pay attention to how it's being said. Phrases like "It seems like you're really concerned about..." or "I hear that you're feeling..." can show customers that their emotions are being noticed and respected. This not only helps clarify their concerns, but also creates a more engaged and empathetic interaction.

- **Customer feedback analysis:** Looking at direct feedback can uncover emotional trends in customer interactions. Tools like sentiment analysis in text-based communication help businesses decode emotional undertones in emails, reviews, and chat transcripts (Sharma, 2025a). Identifying patterns in positive and negative feedback gives companies a clearer picture of what aspects of their service resonate with customers—and what needs improvement.

- **Validating emotions:** Sometimes, all a customer wants is to feel heard. Simple statements like, "I completely understand why this would be upsetting" or "That sounds really frustrating" can de-escalate tensions and build trust. Studies show that when customers feel a genuine emotional connection with a brand, they're more likely to remain loyal and even recommend the company to others (Martinuzzi, 2023).

Training Teams to Respond to Emotional Cues

Recognizing emotional cues is just the first step—knowing how to respond appropriately is what truly sets great customer service apart. That's why training in this area is so valuable. Role-playing exercises, where representatives practice real-world scenarios, can be particularly effective. When team members take on both the role of the customer and the service rep, they gain a deeper appreciation for how emotional responses influence interactions.

For example, imagine a training session where a representative has to handle a customer who received a damaged product. Instead of just focusing on offering a refund or replacement, the exercise would emphasize tone, language, and empathy. Learning to say, "I'm really sorry this happened—we want to make this right for you," with genuine concern, can transform the experience from transactional to personal.

By honing the ability to recognize and respond to emotional cues, customer service teams can turn everyday interactions into meaningful connections that drive loyalty and satisfaction.

Responding Effectively to Emotional Customer Needs

Great customer service depends on recognizing and responding to how customers feel at that moment. Every interaction is an opportunity to connect to show customers that they're not just another ticket number but a valued part of the brand's community. And the key to making that connection? Again, emotional intelligence.

Customers express their emotions in different ways, and a sharp customer service professional knows how to pick up on these cues and adjust their approach accordingly. Someone venting about a delayed order isn't just upset about the package; they might be frustrated because they needed it for an important event. A response like, "I completely understand how this delay must be frustrating for you. Let me check on the status and see what we can do to make it right," immediately acknowledges their emotions before shifting toward a solution. That simple recognition of their frustration makes a huge difference.

The Power of Empathetic Communication

The way a message is delivered matters just as much as the words themselves. A calm, reassuring tone can help soothe an anxious customer, while a warm, upbeat response might lift the spirits of someone having a bad day. Adjusting speech patterns and phrasing to match the customer's emotional state makes interactions feel more human and genuine. It's being present in the conversation and responding with sincerity.

For tougher situations, de-escalation techniques are invaluable. A customer might come in hot, feeling ignored, wronged, or simply exhausted from a long wait. What is the worst thing a service representative can do? Meet their frustration with defensiveness. Instead, staying calm, listening without interrupting, and validating their emotions can turn things around. A phrase like, "I hear you, and I can see why this would be upsetting," shows understanding. Following that up with a concrete step toward a resolution helps shift the focus from frustration to progress. When done well, these techniques don't just resolve the immediate issue—they leave the customer feeling heard and respected.

Great service doesn't stop once the issue is resolved. A follow-up email, a quick check-in call, or even a simple "Hope everything's working out now!" message shows customers that they weren't just a transaction. It tells them that their experience matters. This kind of personalized attention turns satisfied customers into loyal ones—and loyal customers into brand advocates. People appreciate businesses that go the extra mile to ensure they're happy, and they're more likely to return and recommend the brand to others (Borowski, 2024; Perzynska, 2024).

Training Teams to Respond With Emotional Intelligence

Like any skill, responding to emotional needs takes practice. Customer service teams that train in empathy, active listening, and adaptive communication perform better because they're prepared for a range of emotional reactions. Role-playing exercises, for example, help representatives experience both sides of an interaction—giving them a deeper understanding of what customers go through and how to respond effectively. Emotional intelligence training programs that focus on these areas provide teams with the confidence and tools to handle even the most challenging situations with grace.

For small businesses and startups, where every customer interaction carries even more weight, these techniques can be a game-changer. With fewer resources to rely on, small teams have to stand out in other ways—and exceptional, emotionally intelligent service is one of the most powerful differentiators. Creating a culture where customer emotions are acknowledged and valued helps businesses build strong, lasting relationships that drive growth.

Responding to customers' emotional needs enriches the service encounter. When businesses master the art of personalized responses, empathetic communication, de-escalation techniques, and meaningful follow-ups, they create experiences that customers don't just appreciate—they remember. And that's what keeps them coming back.

Conclusion

We've covered a lot in this chapter, but one thing stands out: emotional intelligence is a game-changer. Recognizing and responding to emotions with empathy and care transforms routine interactions into meaningful connections. Whether it's picking up on subtle cues, de-escalating tense situations, or simply making customers feel heard, these skills set the foundation for exceptional service.

For managers, entrepreneurs, and small business owners, investing in emotional intelligence isn't just about improving customer satisfaction—it's about building a service culture that fosters trust, loyalty, and even stronger team morale. When teams feel empowered to engage with customers on a human level, they solve problems, but most importantly, they create experiences that leave a lasting impact. Those personal touches are what turn first-time customers into lifelong advocates.

As we've seen, emotional intelligence is a cornerstone of exceptional service. But how can we take these connections a step further? In the next chapter, we'll explore how to design customer experiences that not only meet expectations but exceed them.

Susan Williamson

Chapter 3: Designing Memorable Customer Experiences

Creating unforgettable customer experiences is both an art and a science—maybe even a little magical. When was the last time a business made you feel like more than just another transaction? Maybe it was the personalized greeting, the thoughtful follow-up, or the way they anticipated exactly what you needed before you even had to ask. That kind of magic doesn't happen by accident; it's the result of understanding customers on a deeper level, being intentional about every touchpoint, and continually refining the experience to exceed expectations.

In this chapter, we're learning what it takes to create experiences that not only meet expectations but also exceed them—turning routine interactions into something unforgettable. From getting to the heart of what customers really want to use technology for smart, seamless personalization, we'll break down the strategies that keep people engaged and coming back for more. You'll discover how to anticipate needs before they're even voiced, fine-tune your approach through real customer feedback, and stay ahead of shifting trends to keep your service fresh, relevant, and irresistible.

By the end of this chapter, you'll have a toolkit of strategies to design experiences that not only meet expectations but also exceed them, creating loyal customers who can't help but come back for more and set your business apart in a competitive marketplace.

Identifying Customer Expectations and Desires

Creating an unforgettable customer experience starts with knowing exactly what your customers want, and let's be honest: their expectations aren't getting any lower. People expect businesses not just to meet their needs but to anticipate them. The companies that stand out are the ones that take the time to understand their audience, refine every interaction, and build systems that keep feedback flowing. It's not about guessing what customers want; it's about listening, adapting, and delivering consistently.

Actionable Strategies

These strategies include:

- **Identifying customer personas:** Not all customers are looking for the same experience, and treating them as if they are is a recipe for mediocrity. Younger customers might prefer a quick, seamless digital experience, while older customers may appreciate a real conversation with a person. Some want speed, others want guidance. By breaking customers into clear personas—based on demographics, behaviors, and preferences—businesses can make their service feel tailored instead of one-size-fits-all. As Wintermantel (2024) points out, factors like past interactions, cultural background, and industry norms shape what people expect from a company. The more a business understands these nuances, the more they can deliver experiences that hit the mark.

- **Customer journey mapping:** Once you know who your customers are, the next step is figuring out how they move through your business. What's their first touchpoint? Where do they get frustrated? What makes them come back—or never return? That's where customer journey mapping comes in. By charting every interaction a customer has with your business, you can spot weak points and fine-tune the experience. Fontanella (2022) emphasizes that journey mapping helps businesses provide smoother, frustration-free service across all channels. Take an online store, for example. If people are abandoning their carts at checkout, something is off—maybe the process is too long, or there aren't enough payment options. Identifying these bottlenecks and fixing them can be the difference between a lost sale and a loyal customer.

- **Implementing feedback mechanisms:** Want to know if you're meeting expectations? Just ask. The best businesses don't guess—they listen.

Customer feedback, whether through surveys, reviews, or direct conversations, gives companies a reality check on what's working and what needs to change. But collecting feedback is only half the equation. Acting on it is what really builds trust. If multiple customers are saying that wait times are too long, for example, addressing it shows that their voices matter. And with AI-powered sentiment analysis, businesses can now track customer reactions in real-time, making it easier than ever to adjust and improve.

- **Analyzing trends:** Staying ahead of customer expectations also means keeping an eye on industry trends. Consumer behavior shifts fast, and companies that anticipate change—rather than react to it—have the advantage. For instance, as sustainability becomes a bigger priority for consumers, businesses that proactively incorporate eco-friendly practices set themselves apart.

Customer journey mapping and structured feedback collection are two of the most effective tools for achieving these goals. A well-executed journey map should highlight key moments like onboarding, purchasing, and support interactions—examining them from the customer's perspective to identify opportunities for improvement. Meanwhile, feedback collection should be intentional and easy for customers to engage with. Simple survey tools, incentives for reviews, or even quick check-ins via email can make all the difference in gathering meaningful insights.

Designing memorable experiences isn't a one-and-done task. It's a continuous process of learning, refining, and staying ahead of the curve. Whether it's mapping out the journey, personalizing interactions, or responding to feedback, the goal is simple: to create experiences so good that customers don't just come back—they bring others with them.

Incorporating Personalization Into Service

Making customers feel like more than just another transaction is what transforms a routine interaction into something meaningful. That's where personalization comes in. Greeting customers by name or remembering their last purchase won't do it; creating experiences that make them feel genuinely seen and understood will. When done well, personalization fosters deeper connections, increases loyalty, and sets a business apart from the competition.

Tools and Strategies for Personalization

- Leverage customer data for tailored experiences. Businesses that analyze customer behavior—like past purchases, browsing history, and service interactions—can offer hyper-targeted recommendations that align with individual preferences. Restaurants, for example, can suggest dishes that a customer has enjoyed before, while e-commerce companies can tailor product recommendations based on previous shopping habits. This kind of thoughtful personalization makes interactions feel seamless and natural, increasing customer satisfaction. But as Zahidi et al. (2024) emphasize, data privacy is crucial—customers need to trust that their personal information is being handled responsibly. When businesses use data ethically and transparently, they strengthen customer confidence, making them more likely to engage with personalized services.

- Offer customizable options to enhance engagement. Giving customers control over their experiences fosters a stronger emotional connection to a brand. Consider how popular coffee chains allow customers to fine-tune their drinks, adjusting everything from milk alternatives to flavor shots. Subscription services apply a similar concept by offering customizable plans tailored to individual preferences. This ability to personalize an order, service, or experience not only increases satisfaction but also reinforces a sense of ownership. Customers feel they're not just another number; they're individuals with unique needs that the business recognizes and respects.

- Use technology to automate and scale personalization. While one-on-one interactions are ideal, businesses need scalable solutions to deliver personalized service at scale. AI-powered tools help by analyzing vast amounts of data in real-time, adapting recommendations and interactions instantly. Streaming platforms, for instance, use sophisticated algorithms to suggest content tailored to individual viewing habits, ensuring users find something they enjoy without endless searching. Chatbots equipped with AI further enhance customer interactions by providing real-time, personalized responses to inquiries. These automated tools ensure that customers receive fast, relevant support while still feeling like their needs are uniquely understood (The FullStory Team, 2024).

- Empower employees to deliver human-centered personalization. Technology can streamline personalization, but human interaction remains irreplaceable. Employees who recognize customer preferences and have the flexibility to tailor their approach can elevate an experience in ways automation cannot. Imagine a hotel employee greeting a returning guest by name and already knowing their pillow preference or a retail associate recalling a loyal customer's style and suggesting a perfect new arrival. These small but meaningful gestures create emotional connections that drive long-term loyalty. Training and empowering employees to go beyond scripted responses and genuinely engage with customers gives businesses a competitive advantage—one that can't be replicated by technology alone.

- Continuously refine personalization strategies through customer feedback. Personalization isn't a onetime effort; it's an ongoing process that evolves alongside customer expectations. Encouraging feedback through surveys, reviews, and direct conversations helps businesses fine-tune their approach. By actively listening to customers and making adjustments based on their insights, companies create a sense of partnership—customers feel heard, and their input helps shape the service they receive. AI-driven sentiment analysis further enhances this process by identifying patterns in customer emotions, allowing businesses to make proactive improvements. A well-maintained feedback loop fosters trust, ensuring that personalization remains relevant, effective, and valued.

Personalization shows customers they matter, not just as buyers but as individuals. Businesses that master this approach create lasting relationships that drive loyalty, advocacy, and long-term success.

Creative Approaches to Enhance Experiences

This crowded marketplace forces businesses to stand out not just by offering good products or services but also by crafting experiences that customers can't stop talking about. The businesses that thrive are the ones that go beyond expectations, adding elements of surprise, delight, and innovation to every interaction. Whether it's through unique service offerings, unexpected gestures, or emotionally engaging storytelling, creativity is a game-changer in customer experience.

Creative Approaches

- **Innovate service offerings:** Customers are drawn to experiences that feel fresh, exciting, and different. Offering something beyond the usual product or service can create an instant competitive edge. A coffee shop that serves great coffee and also provides an immersive virtual reality experience for customers to enjoy while they sip their drinks truly stands out. That extra, unexpected element turns a routine visit into something extraordinary. The key is to think outside the box: What can your business provide that no one else does? Innovation doesn't have to be high tech or expensive—it just has to be meaningful and relevant to your audience. Personally, I had an experience on a charter flight from San Francisco to Atlanta when my clients requested sushi for dinner. I had the finest fish and all the necessary ingredients delivered to the plane at a significant cost. However, when the clients arrived to board the plane, they all had bags of Chik-Fil-A. They explained that they had changed their minds and asked their limo driver to go through the drive-thru because one of the clients had never tried the famous chicken sandwich.

Instead of being frustrated by the change, I adapted quickly. I paired the chicken sandwiches with a perfect Pinot Grigio and served it with the same level of care and attention I would have given to the sushi. The clients were delighted, and the situation turned into a memorable experience.

This experience taught me the importance of flexibility and thinking on my feet. By embracing the unexpected and finding a creative solution, I was able to turn a potential conflict into a positive and unique customer experience.

- **Surprise and delight customers:** Small, unexpected gestures can make a big impact, forging emotional connections that lead to long-term loyalty. A personalized thank-you note, a free sample tailored to past purchases, or an exclusive discount given "just because" can transform an ordinary interaction into a memorable one. According to Iheagwara (2024), exceeding expectations in simple yet thoughtful ways leaves a lasting impression. However, authenticity is key—surprises should feel natural, not forced. Empowering employees to identify moments where they can genuinely delight customers ensures that these experiences remain heartfelt and meaningful rather than gimmicky.

- **Utilize storytelling to build connections:** Stories resonate in ways that facts and figures simply can't. A compelling narrative can help customers relate to your brand on a deeper level, making them feel like part of your journey. Whether it's sharing the inspiration behind your business, highlighting an employee's story, or showcasing how your product has positively impacted a customer's life, storytelling humanizes your brand. When people connect emotionally with a brand's values and mission, they become more than just customers—they become advocates who share your story with others.

- **Celebrate customer milestones:** Acknowledging and celebrating key moments creates a sense of belonging and strengthens relationships. Recognizing birthdays, anniversaries, or even customer loyalty milestones shows that you see them as individuals, not just transactions. Quill Creative Studio emphasizes that leveraging brand milestones fosters excitement and connection (*The Power of Brand Milestones: Leveraging Your Brand's Special Events*, 2023). Whether it's offering a special discount for a long-time customer, hosting an exclusive event for VIP clients, or simply sending a congratulatory message for an achievement, these gestures reinforce customer appreciation and deepen engagement.

While creativity is essential, it's equally important to implement these strategies in a way that feels sustainable and scalable. Surprises should be personalized yet manageable, ensuring they remain impactful without becoming overwhelming for your team. Similarly, milestone celebrations should be spaced thoughtfully to maintain their significance. By integrating these creative elements into your customer experience strategy, you're not just providing a service—you're creating moments that customers will remember and share.

Ensuring Experiences are Emotionally Resonant

A returning customer is a customer that felt something, and it wasn't just efficiency or convenience. Emotions shape how people perceive interactions, influence their decisions, and determine whether they'll stick with a brand or move on. Businesses that tap into emotional engagement build deeper connections, fostering stronger loyalty and long-term success.

Key Strategies for Emotional Engagement

- **Leveraging emotional triggers:** Emotional triggers are key to designing experiences that leave a lasting impact. Joy, surprise, empathy—these emotions turn ordinary interactions into meaningful moments. Picture a boutique hotel welcoming guests with a personalized note and a small, thoughtful gift tailored to their preferences. These unexpected touches create emotional bonds, leaving customers with positive memories that keep them coming back. Thoughtful gestures like these should be embedded into service strategies to consistently evoke positive emotions across every touchpoint.
- **Training staff in emotional intelligence:** A brand's ability to deliver emotionally resonant experiences depends heavily on its frontline employees. That's why investing in emotional intelligence training is critical. Employees who recognize emotional cues can respond with empathy, transforming potential frustrations into positive experiences. Example: A customer is upset about a delayed shipment; an emotionally aware service rep acknowledges the inconvenience, expresses genuine concern, and provides a

proactive solution. This approach resolves the issue and strengthens the customer's trust in the brand. By fostering emotional awareness, businesses empower their teams to turn everyday interactions into moments of genuine connection.

- **Creating emotional touchpoints throughout the journey:** Certain moments in the customer journey—like making a purchase, receiving a product, or dealing with a service issue—carry heightened emotional weight. These are prime opportunities to infuse positive emotions. A handwritten thank-you note with an order, a follow-up call to check on customer satisfaction, or a surprise upgrade for a loyal client can all leave a deep impression. Mapping out these emotional touchpoints helps businesses pinpoint where they can make the biggest impact, ensuring that every stage of the customer journey resonates on a personal level.

- **Gathering and acting on emotional feedback:** Understanding how customers feel about their experiences is just as important as delivering those experiences in the first place. Businesses that actively gather emotional feedback—through sentiment analysis, surveys, or social media monitoring—gain valuable insights into what's working and what needs improvement. If customers frequently express frustration with long wait times, for example, it signals an area that requires immediate attention. By continuously listening and adapting, brands can refine their strategies to better align with customer expectations, ensuring that their emotional impact remains strong.

- **Using emotional scoring to predict and personalize experiences:** Emotional scoring takes customer insights a step further, using data to measure emotional engagement and predict future behaviors. High scores can indicate potential brand advocates, while lower scores highlight areas needing improvement. Businesses can use this information to personalize interactions, such as offering exclusive perks to highly engaged customers or addressing concerns with those who feel disconnected. While technology plays a role in gathering this data, it's the human touch—thoughtful service and genuine care—that brings these insights to life and strengthens customer relationships.

Ultimately, emotionally resonant experiences aren't about grand gestures; they're about meaningful, well-timed interactions that show customers they're valued. A simple yet heartfelt interaction, like a sincere thank-you from a store associate or a personalized follow-up email, can leave a lasting impression. By weaving emotional engagement into everyday service, businesses surpass expectations, creating experiences that customers remember, talk about, and return to time and time again, thereby strengthening brand loyalty in the process.

Conclusion

Creating memorable customer experiences is about crafting moments that leave a lasting impact. And at the heart of it all? Knowing your customers inside and out. When you take the time to understand their needs, expectations, and even their frustrations, you gain the power to design interactions that feel effortless and deeply satisfying. That's why mapping the customer journey is so important. It helps you see things from their perspective, pinpoint areas to enhance and smooth out any bumps along the way. Just as crucial is listening—actively gathering feedback and using it to refine the experience in real-time. When customers see that their input actually shapes the way you operate, they feel valued and engaged in a way that strengthens their connection to your brand.

Great service exceeds expectations in ways that feel personal, meaningful, and surprising. Personalization is a game-changer, whether it's remembering a customer's preferences or using AI-driven insights to anticipate their needs. And while technology helps scale these efforts, it's the human touch that truly makes the difference. Empowering employees to be creative, empathetic, and proactive in their interactions turns routine transactions into standout moments. Layering in emotional resonance—sparking joy, delivering pleasant surprises, or showing genuine empathy—elevates an experience from good to unforgettable. And the key to making it all work is consistently refining and evolving your approach based on ongoing feedback.

Of course, delivering exceptional experiences is only part of the equation. The next step is understanding how to measure their impact. In the next chapter, we'll explore the metrics and tools that help you track customer satisfaction, analyze trends, and make data-driven decisions that fuel long-term success.

Chapter 4: Effective Communication Skills

Let's come back to that memory of a great customer service representative you encountered. What made it stand out? Chances are, it came down to how well that person communicated with you. Effective communication shouldn't aim for only saying the right things, but for making a connection. It's the difference between leaving a conversation feeling frustrated and walking away feeling heard, understood, and valued.

Whether you're answering a question, solving a problem, or just having a friendly chat, the way you communicate can turn an ordinary interaction into something memorable. It's not just about the words you use but how you say them, how you listen, and even the little things like your tone or body language. When done right, communication builds trust, resolves issues, and leaves customers feeling good about their experience.

In this chapter, we're studying the art of communication in customer service. We'll talk about how to deliver clear messages through the phone, when writing an email, or speaking face-to-face. You'll learn why listening empathetically is so important and how it can make customers feel truly heard. We'll also explore the little things—like tone and body language—that can make or break an interaction. By the time you reach the end of this chapter, you'll have a solid set of strategies to make every customer interaction smooth, effective, and, most importantly, memorable. Come with me!

Elements of Clear and Empathetic Communication

Great customer interactions are built on a foundation of clarity and empathy. Think about the last time you asked for help and got a vague or confusing response. Frustrating, right? Now, contrast that with an experience where someone gave you a clear, straightforward answer that actually solved your problem. That's the power of effective communication—it eliminates misunderstandings, fosters trust, and ensures that customers walk away feeling valued and informed.

These are elements that make effective communication:

- **Clarity in messaging:** Clear communication is the backbone of great service. When customers reach out, they want precise, easy-to-understand answers—not a guessing game. Imagine calling a company for help and getting a long-winded, overly technical explanation that leaves you more confused than when you started. Compare that to a support agent who breaks things down simply, guiding you step by step. The difference? Clarity ensures customers feel confident in their next steps rather than overwhelmed.

This applies to written communication, too. Whether it's an email, chat support, or an FAQ section, using direct and concise language eliminates unnecessary complexity. Jargon-free messaging is especially important for customers from diverse backgrounds, ensuring accessibility and ease of understanding. A well-written response not only answers the question but also reassures the customer that they're in good hands.

- **Empathetic listening:** Communication it's also about how well you listen and not just talk. Empathetic listening means fully tuning in to what the customer is saying (and not saying) to understand their needs, emotions, and concerns. Imagine a customer calling with a complaint. A rushed or indifferent response will only add to their frustration. But an agent who actively listens acknowledges the issue and responds with genuine care can turn a negative situation into a positive one.

Simple actions like maintaining eye contact, nodding, or using phrases like "I understand" or "That sounds frustrating—let me help" reassure customers that their concerns matter. When customers feel heard, they're more likely to trust the resolution process and walk away with a better impression of the business.

- **Feedback mechanisms:** Customer feedback is perhaps the most important element. Encouraging customers to share their thoughts not only helps improve service but also strengthens their connection to the brand. Think about a small café where regulars suggest menu tweaks or service improvements. When the café owner listens and makes changes based on those insights, it signals to customers that their opinions matter. This kind of feedback loop fosters loyalty and ensures the business keeps evolving in ways that truly meet customer expectations.

  But only collecting feedback is not enough, businesses need to act on it. A simple "Thank you for your suggestion! We've taken your input and made this improvement" closes the loop and shows customers they have a voice in shaping their experience. That kind of engagement builds long-term trust and keeps customers coming back.

- **Non-verbal cues and tone:** Communication isn't just verbal. Your body language, facial expressions, and tone of voice all play a huge role in how messages are received. A service rep who avoids eye contact crosses their arms, or speaks in a monotone voice is giving a message beyond their spoken words. Even with the right words, their demeanor might make a customer feel dismissed or unimportant. Now, imagine someone who leans in slightly, maintains an open posture, and speaks in a warm, engaging tone. The difference is night and day.

The tone of voice is just as important. A friendly, calm tone invites openness, while a harsh or impatient one can instantly put a customer on edge. Even simple word choices, like saying "I'd be happy to help" instead of "That's not my department," can shift the entire feel of an interaction.

And let's not forget cultural sensitivity—what's considered polite body language in one culture might come off as distant or aggressive in another. Being mindful of these nuances helps avoid miscommunication and ensures every customer feels respected, no matter their background.

Mastering clear and empathetic communication means blending all these elements—clarity, active listening, feedback, and nonverbal awareness—into every customer interaction. When done well, it doesn't just solve problems; it builds relationships, strengthens loyalty, and turns everyday conversations into memorable experiences.

Conflict Resolution Techniques in Customer Service

Customer service representatives are bound to face conflict eventually, so conflict handling is a key skill. A well-managed resolution can turn a frustrated customer into a loyal one. Instead of seeing conflicts as setbacks, think of them as opportunities to build trust and improve service.

Here's a step-by-step approach to resolving customer conflicts effectively:

1. **Identify the root cause:** Every conflict has an underlying issue, and getting to the heart of it is the first step toward resolution. This starts with actively listening to the customer—without interruption—to fully understand their frustration. Giving them the space to express their concerns not only provides clarity but also helps defuse heightened emotions (Cerdeira, 2018). Asking open-ended questions like, "Can you walk me through what happened before this issue arose?" encourages the customer to share important details. This deeper insight ensures that the resolution addresses the real issue, not just the symptoms.

2. **Use "I" statements to communicate understanding:** Once the issue is clear, framing

responses with "I" statements helps create a non-confrontational atmosphere. Instead of assigning blame, this technique expresses concern and a commitment to a solution. For example, saying, "I feel concerned when we don't meet your expectations because we truly value your satisfaction," reassures the customer that their issue is being taken seriously while keeping the conversation collaborative (Roosa, 2024). Using this approach helps prevent defensive reactions and keeps the focus on resolving the issue rather than placing fault.

3. **Brainstorm solutions together:** Customers appreciate being part of the resolution process—it gives them a sense of control and investment in the outcome. A simple question like, "What would an ideal resolution look like for you?" can open the door to finding a solution that works for both sides. This collaborative approach not only increases customer satisfaction but can also uncover innovative ideas. Customers often have unique insights based on their experiences, and their suggestions may lead to process improvements that benefit future interactions. Companies that embrace flexibility and customer input demonstrate adaptability, which strengthens trust and brand loyalty.

4. **Implement and follow through:** Once a solution is agreed upon, it's crucial to act on it promptly and efficiently. Clear communication

about the next steps—such as expected timelines or necessary follow-ups—sets the right expectations and reassures the customer that their issue is being handled. However, resolving a conflict doesn't end with implementing the solution. A follow-up email or call ensures that everything has been fully addressed. A simple message like, "We wanted to check in and make sure everything is now to your satisfaction," reinforces the company's commitment to service beyond the initial interaction.

5. **Seek feedback for continuous improvement:** Every resolved conflict is a learning opportunity. By gathering feedback from customers post-resolution, companies can assess how effective their solutions are and identify areas for improvement. This proactive approach transforms conflict resolution from a reactive process into an ongoing strategy for service enhancement. Customers who see their feedback leading to tangible improvements feel valued, making them more likely to remain loyal in the long run.

Mastering these conflict resolution techniques not only helps resolve immediate issues but also strengthens long-term relationships with customers. When done right, even the most difficult situations can become moments that reinforce trust, professionalism, and exceptional service.

Utilizing Effective Tone and Body Language

Nonverbal communication plays a massive role in customer interactions—sometimes, what's left unsaid speaks louder than words. The way you use your tone, body language, and nonverbal cues can either build trust or create barriers. Customers pick up on subtle signals, whether it's your posture, eye contact, or even the energy in your voice. Here's how to ensure your message comes across the way you intend.

Here are the elements of tone and body language to take into account when communicating with customers:

- **The role of tone variation:** Your tone sets the stage for the entire conversation. It's not just about *what* you say, but *how* you say it. A warm, welcoming tone invites customers into the interaction, making them feel valued and respected, while a flat, rushed, or impatient tone can make them feel like an inconvenience. Imagine calling a customer service line and hearing a cheerful *"Good morning! How can I assist you today?"* versus a robotic *"Yeah, what do you need?"* The words might technically offer help, but the second version makes the customer feel unwelcome.

Studies show that nearly 40% of a message's impact comes from vocal elements like tone, pace, and inflection (University of Texas, 2020). A rushed or monotone voice can create distance, while a steady, expressive tone fosters connection. The key is balance—matching your tone to the situation.

Customer service leaders can help their teams refine their tone by encouraging self-awareness and practice. Listening to recorded calls or role-playing different scenarios can highlight areas for improvement. The goal is to create an emotional connection through speech, ensuring customers feel genuinely heard.

- **The role of body language:** Even when no words are spoken, your body sends a message. A closed-off stance, crossed arms, or lack of eye contact can make customers feel ignored or dismissed. On the flip side, an open posture engaged eye contact, and active listening gestures—like nodding or leaning in slightly—show attentiveness and respect.

Research suggests that people who smile are perceived as more approachable and trustworthy (University of Texas, 2020). A sincere smile, paired with a welcoming posture, immediately puts customers at ease. Similarly, subtle hand gestures can reinforce what's being said, making explanations clearer and more engaging.

However, body language should always align with the spoken message. Small inconsistencies can damage credibility and leave customers feeling dismissed. Practicing self-awareness in front of a mirror or recording interactions can help professionals refine their nonverbal cues to ensure they always reinforce a positive customer experience.

- **Mirroring techniques:** One of the most effective (yet underutilized) techniques in customer service is mirroring. When done naturally, mirroring a customer's tone, energy level, or body language creates an instant sense of connection. This psychological phenomenon makes people feel understood and comfortable in interactions.

  For example, if a customer speaks slowly and softly, responding in the same manner conveys calmness and understanding. If a customer is more energetic and enthusiastic, mirroring that enthusiasm builds rapport. The key is subtlety—overly obvious imitation can feel artificial and off-putting. Instead, slight adjustments in speech patterns, gestures, or even facial expressions can make the interaction feel more in sync.

- **Cultural sensitivity in nonverbal communication:** While body language and tone play universal roles in communication, their interpretation varies widely across cultures. A gesture that is perfectly acceptable in one country might be misunderstood or even offensive in another. For example, maintaining direct eye contact is a sign of confidence and honesty in many Western cultures, but in some Asian cultures, it can be seen as confrontational or disrespectful.

Businesses that interact with globally diverse customer bases must educate their teams about these differences to avoid misunderstandings. Training sessions, cultural competency workshops, and simply asking customers about their preferences can go a long way in fostering respectful and effective communication.

Encouraging open discussions about cultural norms within customer service teams helps to build awareness and sensitivity. When in doubt, observing a customer's body language and mirroring their level of formality can be a safe approach. The goal is to create an inclusive and comfortable experience for every customer, regardless of their background.

Mastering these nonverbal elements ensures that your message is not only heard, but also felt in a way that strengthens customer relationships.

Overcoming Communication

Barriers

Clear, effective communication is the foundation of great customer service. But let's be real—barriers pop up all the time. Whether it's technical issues, cultural misunderstandings, or just plain frustration, these roadblocks can turn a simple conversation into a stressful ordeal. The good news? With the right strategies, you can navigate these challenges and keep the dialogue flowing smoothly.

Step 1: Identifying Communication Barriers

The first step to fixing a problem is recognizing it. Communication barriers come in different forms, and each requires a unique approach:

- **Physical barriers:** Ever tried having a conversation over a crackling phone line? It's frustrating—for both sides. Poor audio quality, bad internet connections, or even background noise can make it difficult to understand each other. These issues might seem minor, but they can quickly escalate into bigger frustrations if not addressed.
- **Cultural barriers:** In today's global marketplace, cultural differences can lead to misunderstandings.

A phrase that's perfectly normal in one language might not translate well into another, and gestures or tones of voice can have different meanings across cultures. Without awareness of these nuances, even well-intentioned messages can be misinterpreted, leading to confusion or even offense. For example, I was raised in Redondo Beach, California, and moved to the South at age fourteen. I was taken aback by the Southern accent and had a hard time understanding it for years. One day, while working at an FBO (Fixed Base Operator), a lady complimented me on my mascara. Then, she asked me, "What close your eyes, honey?" I asked her to repeat the question, and she did, "What close your eyes?" I didn't understand why she wanted me to close my eyes, but I did. I stood there, representing the company I worked for, and closed my eyes as the customer requested. There was complete silence for a minute, and then my co-worker nudged me and said, "She is asking what color your eyes are!" Dumbfounded, I opened my eyes and said, "Oh, they are brown. I have brown eyes." I laughed, embarrassed.

This experience taught me how easily communication can break down, even over something as simple as an accent. It's a reminder that patience, active listening, and a willingness to clarify can go a long way in bridging gaps and avoiding misunderstandings.

- **Emotional barriers:** Stress, frustration, or even just a bad day can cloud communication. An upset customer might struggle to articulate their issue clearly, while a stressed-out service rep might unintentionally come across as dismissive. Emotions shape interactions, and without careful handling, they can become a barrier to resolution.

Step 2: Simplify Language

Jargon might make you sound like an expert, but it can also leave customers completely lost. Industry-specific terms and acronyms can alienate people who aren't familiar with them, making interactions more confusing than they need to be.

The fix? Keep it simple. Instead of saying, "Our API integrates seamlessly with your ERP," try, "Our systems work well together with yours." Clarity is key. The goal is to ensure that every customer—regardless of their technical background—understands exactly what you're saying.

A great habit to develop is rephrasing technical explanations in everyday language. If a customer seems confused, take a step back and ask yourself, "How would I explain this to someone with no industry experience?" This approach keeps customers engaged, informed, and confident in the service they're receiving.

Step 3: Practice Patience and Understanding

Customers don't always have the words to describe their issues right away, and that's okay. Rushing them through an explanation only adds to their frustration. Instead, patience is your best tool. Giving customers the space to express themselves—without interruptions—helps them feel heard and understood.

But patience alone isn't enough; empathy is what truly transforms the interaction. Simple phrases like "I completely understand how that must feel" or "That sounds frustrating—I'd feel the same way" can go a long way in diffusing tension. When customers feel acknowledged, they're more likely to work with you rather than against you.

Patience and understanding don't just resolve the immediate issue—they also build trust. A customer who feels respected and valued is far more likely to stay loyal to your brand.

Step 4: Leverage Technology Wisely

Technology can be a game-changer for overcoming communication barriers—when used wisely.

- **Translation tools:** Whether it's a translation app or built-in multilingual support, these tools make it easier to serve customers who speak different languages. Real-time translation services allow for smoother, more inclusive conversations, ensuring that no customer feels left out due to a language barrier.

- **Video conferencing:** Sometimes, tone and body language makes all the difference. Video chats add an extra layer of communication that's missing in emails or phone calls. A reassuring smile or a nod of understanding can help ease tensions and reinforce that the customer is being heard.

- **Reliability matters:** The best technology in the world is useless if it doesn't work properly. Outdated software, slow response times, or glitchy chatbots can do more harm than good. Keeping tech tools updated and ensuring they actually enhance the customer experience is just as important as having them in the first place.

By integrating these strategies into everyday interactions, businesses can break down communication barriers and create more meaningful, productive conversations. Whether it's recognizing the obstacles, simplifying language, showing patience, or leveraging technology, each step contributes to a stronger, more trust-filled relationship with customers.

Conclusion

With all the knowledge imparted in this chapter, it's clear that mastering communication skills is a game-changer for customer interactions. We've explored the importance of clear messaging—how straightforward information leaves customers feeling satisfied and informed. We've also talked about empathetic listening, a skill that helps us connect on a deeper level by truly understanding and valuing what customers have to say. Add in feedback mechanisms, positive body language, and an awareness of cultural differences, and you've got a toolkit to handle any conversation with confidence.

These strategies don't just improve customer service; they strengthen relationships across the board. By focusing on tone, overcoming barriers, and making every customer feel heard and respected, you're setting the stage for meaningful connections. This chapter isn't just about ideas; it's packed with practical tools you can use every day to transform how your team interacts with customers.

As you move forward, keep these techniques in mind. Whether it's simplifying language, practicing patience, or leveraging technology, these skills will help you build stronger relationships and create loyal customers. And speaking of building relationships, in the next chapter, we'll explore how to measure and analyze customer satisfaction, giving you the tools to track your success and keep improving.

Chapter 5: Integrating Technology With Human Touch

Technology has revolutionized customer service, making interactions faster, more efficient, and more accessible. But no matter how advanced automation becomes, customers still crave human connection. The challenge? Striking the right balance between leveraging technology for efficiency and preserving the warmth, empathy, and personalization that define great service. It's not about choosing one over the other; it's about blending both seamlessly to create an experience that is both high-tech and high-touch.

This chapter unpacks the intricate relationship between technology and human interaction in customer service. You'll explore how businesses can harness digital tools to streamline operations, reduce response times, and enhance accessibility—all without making customers feel like they're just another ticket in the system. So, how do businesses walk this tightrope? This chapter also delves into strategies for maintaining personal connections while embracing technological advancements.

Whether you're a customer service manager aiming to refine your team's approach, an entrepreneur looking to scale service without sacrificing quality, or simply someone passionate about creating meaningful customer experiences, this chapter will equip you with the insights and strategies needed to merge technology with human touch effectively. Because at the end of the day, the best customer service doesn't come from choosing between tech and humanity—it comes from knowing how to make them work together.

Advantages and Limitations of Technology in Service

Technology in customer service is a double-edged sword—it can be the biggest improvement when used effectively, but it also presents challenges that need careful management. Striking the right balance between automation and human interaction is key to ensuring that technology enhances, rather than hinders, the customer experience. Let's break it down into the major advantages and limitations.

Enhanced Efficiency

- Technology has revolutionized service efficiency by streamlining processes, reducing wait times, and minimizing human error.
- AI-powered chatbots and automated response systems can handle standard inquiries instantly,

allowing human agents to focus on more complex issues.

- Automation reduces the likelihood of mistakes in routine tasks, enhancing service reliability and consistency.
- By leveraging technology to handle repetitive tasks, businesses free up their staff to provide deeper, more meaningful interactions with customers, improving both service quality and employee job satisfaction.

24/7 Availability

- One of the biggest advantages of technology is its ability to provide round-the-clock customer support.
- Automated systems, such as virtual assistants and AI chatbots, ensure that customers receive immediate responses at any time of day.
- This is especially valuable for businesses with a global clientele, as customers across different time zones can access support without delays.
- Offering continuous service availability can significantly enhance customer engagement and satisfaction, giving businesses a competitive edge in fast-paced markets.

Technology has revolutionized service efficiency by streamlining processes, reducing wait times, and minimizing human error. However, it's important to remember that human judgment and accountability are still crucial in ensuring that these systems are used correctly.

For example, although I don't fly full-time, aviation is a passion of mine. I love everything about it—the smell of jet fuel, the sound of the engines, the feeling of flying, and being around positive people.

However, I once made a mistake I'll never repeat. As a new flight attendant, I poured coffee down the galley drain, not realizing that only clear liquids should go there. Colored liquids like coffee, wine, or juice can stain the exterior of the plane as they drain during flight and even cause mechanical issues. I was embarrassed and didn't want to tell the pilots, but I knew I had to own up to it.

This experience taught me a valuable lesson about accountability and the importance of human judgment, even in environments where technology and systems are heavily relied upon. It also reinforced the need for thorough training and clear communication in high-stakes environments like aviation.

AI-powered chatbots and automated response systems can handle standard inquiries instantly, allowing human agents to focus on more complex issues. Automation reduces the likelihood of mistakes in routine tasks, enhancing service reliability and consistency. By leveraging technology to handle repetitive tasks, businesses free up their staff to provide deeper, more meaningful interactions with customers, improving both service quality and employee job satisfaction.

Personalization Challenges

- While technology improves efficiency, it can sometimes make interactions feel impersonal.
- Automated systems, no matter how advanced, lack the empathy and nuance that human agents bring to interactions.
- Customers with unique or complex issues may find chatbots frustrating when they don't fit neatly into pre-programmed responses.
- Research suggests that while smart technologies can enhance customer experience, businesses must ensure they don't detach from the consumer's extended self (Riegger et al., 2022). For example, customers may prefer personalized offers on their own devices rather than through retailer-owned screens.
- To prevent depersonalization, companies need to strike a balance between automation and human touch, ensuring that customers always have access to a real person when needed.

Data Management and Privacy Concerns

- Technology generates vast amounts of customer data, which can be a goldmine for businesses looking to tailor services and anticipate customer needs.
- Properly analyzed data helps companies personalize interactions, improving overall customer experience and fostering loyalty.
- However, data collection and storage come with significant privacy concerns. Customers are increasingly wary of how their personal information is used.
- Businesses must implement stringent data protection policies and transparent communication practices to maintain customer trust.
- Striking the right balance between utilizing data for improved service and ensuring privacy compliance is essential for long-term success.

Technology is a powerful tool in customer service, but it's not a one-size-fits-all solution. While it boosts efficiency, ensures 24/7 availability, and provides valuable data insights, it also risks depersonalizing interactions and raising privacy concerns. Businesses that successfully integrate technology while preserving the human touch will create more engaging, trustworthy, and customer-centric experiences. The key is continuous evaluation and adaptation to evolving customer expectations and technological advancements.

Selecting the Right Tools for Your Service Model

Picking the right technology just to keep up with trends is a bad idea. When making choices, the aim should be to actually improve customer interactions and streamline operations. The challenge? Finding tools that work *for* your business, not against it. Too much tech can overcomplicate things, while the wrong tools can create more problems than they solve. The goal is to strike that perfect balance—integrating technology in a way that enhances, rather than hinders, the human element of service.

Steps to Aligning Technology With Business Goals

1. **Selecting the right tools:** First, make sure the technology aligns with your service goals. It's easy to get swept up in the latest innovations, but if a tool doesn't directly contribute to improving

customer interactions or operational efficiency, it's just an expensive distraction. For example, if your primary objective is to speed up response times, investing in AI-driven chatbots or automated email responders makes sense. Research from *Strategic Alignment - the Ultimate Guide* (2019) suggests that strategic alignment plays a significant role in determining an organization's success. Simply put, technology should serve your business—not the other way around.

2. **Prioritizing user-friendliness:** Once you've identified tools that fit your needs, usability should be the next priority. A system that's difficult to navigate, whether for customers or employees, will quickly become a bottleneck rather than a solution. No one wants to spend hours deciphering a complicated interface just to get a simple answer. Imagine an e-commerce site with a sophisticated order tracking system—if customers find it confusing to use, it defeats the purpose. The best technology feels effortless, guiding users seamlessly rather than creating roadblocks. Intuitive design, clear navigation, and accessible support resources all contribute to better adoption and satisfaction.

3. **Ensuring integration capabilities:** Integration is another factor. Your tools need to work well together. A Customer Relationship Management (CRM) system that doesn't sync

with your email or customer support platform forces teams to jump between multiple systems, slowing everything down. Disconnected technology doesn't just frustrate employees—it leads to a disjointed customer experience. That's why businesses opt for platforms like Salesforce, which integrate smoothly with various other tools, ensuring a continuous flow of data and information. The smoother the integration, the easier it is to maintain consistency in service delivery.

4. **Conducting a cost-benefit analysis :** Of course, any tech investment also needs to make financial sense. It's not just about the upfront cost but the long-term return on investment. A cutting-edge customer service platform might have a hefty price tag, but if it boosts efficiency, reduces errors, and enhances customer satisfaction, the benefits often outweigh the costs. Toyota's approach to strategic alignment and lean manufacturing (Sourabh-Hajela, 2024) underscores this principle—carefully selecting technology based on both cost and long-term value is key to staying competitive. Businesses should evaluate not just whether a tool is affordable today but whether it will continue delivering value as customer expectations and service demands evolve.

The right technology should feel like an extension of your service model, seamlessly enhancing interactions without overshadowing the personal connections that drive loyalty. By focusing on alignment, usability, integration, and cost-effectiveness, businesses can ensure they're not just adopting technology for the sake of it but using it to create meaningful, customer-centric experiences.

Maintaining Personal Connections With Tech Integration

Blending technology with human connection is one of the trickiest balancing acts in customer service. On one side, tech speeds things up, makes service scalable, and keeps businesses running efficiently. But on the other? Customers still crave meaningful, *human* interactions. The key is using it in a way that enhances, rather than replaces, the personal touch that keeps customers coming back.

So, how do you make that happen?

- **Empower employees to make tech work for them:** One of the best ways to maintain a personal connection is by giving employees the right tools to personalize interactions. When staff members have access to customer histories, they're anticipating their needs.

Beyond just access to data, employees should have opportunities to develop skills that help them navigate tech-driven service. Training in areas like data management and prompt engineering helps them better leverage automation while keeping the experience warm and personal. Human-in-the-loop (HITL) systems also play a huge role here. These systems allow employees to guide AI by providing feedback, ensuring that automation doesn't just run on autopilot but actually improves over time with human insight. And the best part? Empowered employees are more engaged and satisfied in their roles (Execs In The Know, 2024).

- **Make human oversight an easy, seamless process:** No customer wants to feel like they're stuck talking to a machine with no escape route. That's why it's crucial to design service systems where escalating to a human is simple and intuitive. Sure, AI can handle a ton of inquiries efficiently, but when things get complicated, people want to talk to *people*.

The best transitions from automation to human support happen so smoothly that customers barely notice. At the same time, employees should have access to customer interactions with automation so they can pick up where the bot left off instead of making the customer start over.

The real magic happens when human judgment works *with* technology, not against it. AI can sift through data and offer insights, but it's human empathy and emotional intelligence that truly make a difference. That's why businesses that keep human oversight front and center in their tech strategy create stronger, more authentic customer relationships.

- **Use feedback loops to stay ahead of customer needs:** Want to know if your service model is working? Just ask your customers. Gathering real-time insights through surveys, reviews, and interactive feedback features (think thumbs-up/thumbs-down buttons or quick star ratings) helps businesses fine-tune their service strategy. But collecting feedback isn't enough—*acting on it* is what matters.

  By regularly analyzing feedback, businesses can spot patterns, identify pain points, and adapt quickly. Maybe customers love a new self-service option, but they're struggling to find it. Or perhaps an AI-powered recommendation system is off the mark, suggesting irrelevant products. Paying attention to both praise and complaints helps refine these tools, making them more intuitive and customer-friendly. The smartest businesses take it a step further—when customers see their feedback being implemented, it builds trust and loyalty (Subhashis, 2024).

- **Create emotional impact—because connection still matters:** Technology can't replace genuine human connection. Sure, it can assist—suggesting responses, providing context, or streamlining workflows—but the *real* impact comes from how employees engage with customers. That means training teams on tech and emotional intelligence—things like recognizing frustration, practicing active listening, and responding with empathy.

For instance, when a customer reaches out with a complaint, the difference between "Let me look into that for you" and "I completely understand how frustrating that must be—I'm going to fix this for you right away" is huge. The second response builds trust. It acknowledges emotions before jumping into problem-solving.

And yes, tech can assist here, too—by flagging emotionally charged messages for priority escalation or suggesting responses that emphasize empathy. But no matter how advanced AI gets, customers will always remember how a company *made them feel.* Businesses that encourage employees to lean into patience, adaptability, and understanding will always stand out in a world where automation is becoming the norm.

The real secret to maintaining personal connections while integrating technology? Don't think of it as an either-or decision. The best customer experiences happen when tech is used strategically—enhancing efficiency, making jobs easier, and supporting personalization—without ever overshadowing the human element. Businesses that get this balance right don't just serve customers; they build relationships that last.

Evaluating Technological Impact on Customer Service

Integrating technology into customer service is a must. But how do you know if it's actually improving the experience rather than just adding flashy tools that don't move the needle? That's where evaluation comes in. Keeping a pulse on how well your tech-driven strategies are working ensures that you are not only keeping up with trends but also actually delivering better service.

Here are the evaluation tools:

- **Tracking the right performance metrics:** You can't improve what you don't measure. That's why tracking Key Performance Indicators (KPIs) is essential. These metrics—like response times, resolution rates, and customer satisfaction scores—help businesses see what's working and where the gaps are. If automated chat is speeding things up but frustrating customers, that's a sign something needs tweaking. The goal isn't just efficiency; it's effectiveness.

- **Leveraging customer feedback for improvement:** Numbers tell part of the story, but customers will tell you the rest—if you ask. Surveys, feedback forms, and direct conversations help gauge whether your technology is meeting customer expectations. Companies like Euro Systems IT actively collect customer insights to refine their tech integrations, ensuring their systems enhance, rather than hinder, the experience (Ferrie, 2024).
- **Conducting regular service quality assessments:** Just because a system is running smoothly doesn't mean it's delivering real value. Regular service audits—checking system performance, reviewing AI-driven interactions, and assessing ease of use—help ensure technology is doing its job. A great tool that frustrates customers or confuses employees isn't really great at all. Fine-tuning these elements helps maintain high standards and, more importantly, customer trust.
- **Embracing continuous improvement:** The digital world moves fast, and customer expectations evolve just as quickly. A tech solution that works today might be outdated tomorrow. That's why businesses need a culture of continuous improvement—evaluating existing tools, exploring

new trends, and making adjustments along the way. AI-powered chatbots, for example, can be fantastic time-savers, but they should be regularly updated to improve accuracy and handoff efficiency.

- **Blending automation with human connection:** Tech should never replace human interaction—it should enhance it. Live chat, for example, works best when it offers real-time support while smoothly escalating to human agents when needed (Talebi & Bardsiri, 2023). The key is using technology as an enabler, not a substitute for empathy and personal engagement.

- **Empowering employees to use tech effectively:** Even the best technology won't deliver results if employees don't know how to use it well. Training staff on new tools, gathering their feedback, and giving them the confidence to blend automation with personal service is critical. When employees feel equipped, they can focus on what really matters—creating meaningful, personalized interactions that customers appreciate.

- **Aligning technology with business goals:** Technology should serve a purpose, not just be an expensive add-on. Small businesses, in particular, need to be strategic, choosing tools that directly support business objectives without unnecessary complexity. Seamless integration, ease of use, and a clear return on investment should always be a part of the equation.

Technology is a powerful force in customer service—but only when it's thoughtfully implemented, regularly evaluated, and seamlessly blended with the human touch. The businesses that get this right? They're the ones that stand out, delivering service that's both high-tech and high-heart.

Conclusion

In this chapter, we've explored the dance between technology and personal service interactions in the customer service world. It's all about finding that sweet spot where tech and humans work hand-in-hand to make customers happy. We've looked at the power of automated systems like chatbots that keep things going 24/7, making sure no customer is left hanging, no matter the time zone. But we've also seen how too much tech can make things a bit cold and impersonal. That's where the magic of the human touch comes in—employees who know your name, remember your stories and really care about solving your problems.

For those managing customer service teams or driving small businesses forward, the key takeaway is balance. Technology should be like a trusty sidekick, speeding up processes and handling easy stuff so your team can focus on connecting with customers in meaningful ways. This means picking the right tools that fit your goals and getting everyone on board with using them. It's about keeping an eye on what works and being open to change when it doesn't. By mixing tech with heart, you ensure that your customers always feel valued, making those service moments count.

In the next chapter, we'll learn how to measure and analyze customer satisfaction, giving you the tools to track your success and keep improving.

Chapter 6: Frameworks for Customer Service Success

Building a customer service framework is like creating a recipe for success—it's about mixing the right ingredients to create experiences that leave customers smiling and coming back for more. It's not just about answering questions; it's about making every interaction feel personal, consistent, and downright delightful. Think of it as setting up a system where every touchpoint, no matter who handles it, feels like it was designed just for the customer.

In this chapter, we'll explore how to build a framework that works for your business. We'll talk about setting clear goals, standardizing processes, and using performance metrics to keep things on track. You'll also learn why continuous training is so important—it's what keeps your team sharp and ready to handle whatever comes their way.

This chapter is packed with practical tips to help you create a service strategy that's as unique as your business—no matter the size. Let's get started!

Framework

A well-designed customer service framework is the foundation for delivering consistently excellent service. It ensures every interaction supports business goals, maintains quality across channels, and empowers employees to provide meaningful customer experiences. Here's what makes a framework truly effective:

- **Setting clear objectives :** A strong framework starts with well-defined objectives that align customer interactions with broader business goals. These objectives serve as guideposts, helping teams focus on measurable outcomes. Instead of vague aspirations like "improve service," setting specific targets—such as boosting customer satisfaction scores by 10% within six months—creates a clear direction. This clarity fosters accountability and ensures that every action contributes to the bigger picture.

- **Standardizing processes:** Without standardized processes, service quality can vary wildly depending on the channel, the agent, or even the time of day. Customers don't want different answers depending on who they talk to; they want consistency. Imagine a retail brand handling inquiries via phone, email, and chat—without clear guidelines, responses could be disjointed, leading to frustration. Documenting best practices, response templates, and escalation procedures ensures that customers receive the same level of service no matter how they reach out.

- **Tracking performance metrics:** To improve service, you have to measure it. Performance metrics provide a reality check on how well service frameworks are working. Metrics like resolution time, customer feedback ratings, and repeat inquiries offer valuable insights into efficiency and effectiveness. Regularly tracking KPIs—such as Net Promoter Score (NPS) or Customer Satisfaction Score (CSAT)—allows teams to spot trends, identify bottlenecks, and refine strategies. As Peterka (2024) notes, clear and measurable performance indicators help businesses stay aligned with their goals and continuously improve service delivery.

- **Investing in training and resources :** Even the best-designed framework falls apart if employees don't have the knowledge and tools to execute it. Continuous training—whether in soft skills like conflict resolution or technical skills like using a CRM—ensures that service teams are always prepared. Interactive learning, such as role-playing scenarios, reinforces concepts in real-time. Beyond training, easy access to a centralized knowledge base helps employees find quick answers, making them more confident and efficient in their roles. A well-supported team translates into a better experience for customers.

Whenever I train an employee, past or present, I always make sure to address areas for improvement with a balanced approach. An old manager taught me to use two positives and a negative, and I'm forever grateful for that lesson.

For instance, if an employee is struggling with explaining a contract to a customer, I would say, *"I think you're doing a great job answering the phones, and I love your enthusiasm, but let's go over the contract one more time to make sure you understand it and if you have any questions."*

This way, the employee receives two compliments and one area to work on, rather than hearing, *"You need to work on understanding the contract."*

This approach not only builds confidence but also fosters a culture of growth and improvement. It ensures that feedback is constructive and empathetic, which is essential for maintaining morale and encouraging development.

- **Updating the framework:** Customer expectations evolve, and service frameworks should, too. Regular reviews and refinements—based on customer feedback, employee insights, and performance data—help businesses stay ahead of the curve. As highlighted in *Process Frameworks* (n.d.), an adaptable approach ensures service quality keeps pace with industry trends and customer needs.

By combining clear objectives, standardized processes, meaningful metrics, ongoing training, and a commitment to improvement, businesses can build a customer service framework that doesn't just work—it thrives.

Developing Customizable Service Frameworks

Customer service is dynamic. This means that what works today might be outdated tomorrow. Different industries, changing market trends, and evolving customer expectations all demand flexibility. Hence, businesses need a framework that's both effective and adaptable.

Understanding What Your Business Really Needs

A strong service framework starts with knowing exactly what customers expect and how the business operates. A deep dive into service priorities, potential gaps, and areas for improvement is key. A high-end hotel might focus on concierge service, while an e-commerce brand prioritizes fast response times and seamless digital interactions. Recognizing these differences ensures the framework aligns with real customer needs—not just generic best practices.

Beyond shaping a better service model, this process builds confidence among employees. When service teams operate within a structure designed for actual customer needs, they can deliver more consistent, high-quality experiences. Plus, identifying service gaps early prevents small issues from turning into bigger problems (Luck, 2024).

Designing a Framework That Can Evolve

Once businesses understand their priorities, the next step is creating a framework that can adapt. Markets shift. Technology advances. Customer expectations change. A rigid framework can quickly become a liability.

Take, for example, a small bakery that originally focused on in-store sales but pivoted to online orders and curbside pickup. What started as a temporary fix became a long-term strategy. If their service framework had been too rigid, making this shift would have been much harder.

An adaptable framework makes it easier to refine policies, update workflows, and tweak engagement strategies. Whether it's keeping up with customer behavior, rolling out new technology, or responding to economic shifts, flexibility helps businesses stay ahead instead of scrambling to catch up (Bridges, 2024).

Using Feedback to Keep the Framework Relevant

Even the best service framework can become outdated without input from customers and employees. Frontline staff often spot inefficiencies before they escalate, while customers provide direct insight into what's working and what isn't.

Keeping feedback flowing is key. Customer surveys, employee check-ins, and real-time service analytics help pinpoint areas for improvement. Prioritizing this feedback ensures the framework stays practical and customer-focused.

For example, an online retailer might see that email response times are too slow. Employees report that they're overwhelmed because they lack automation tools. Looking at both perspectives makes it clear that the issue isn't just staffing—it's technology. Addressing the root cause strengthens the entire framework, improving efficiency and service quality.

Making Small, Ongoing Improvements

A strong service framework isn't something businesses build once and never touch again—it needs continuous refinement. Instead of waiting for a major overhaul, companies that make small, ongoing improvements keep their service strategies fresh and effective.

Think of a financial services firm that updates its digital support channels each year based on customer behavior and new regulations. Rather than overhauling everything at once, they make steady improvements—enhancing chatbots, refining self-service options, or improving security. These continuous updates keep the framework relevant and aligned with customer expectations.

To maintain momentum, businesses should schedule regular framework reviews. These structured check-ins help assess what's working, analyze feedback, and make proactive adjustments instead of reacting to problems too late.

The Four Keys to a Customizable Service Framework

For businesses looking to build a flexible, future-proof service framework, four key principles stand out:

- **Assess unique needs:** Understand what makes your business and customers distinct, and tailor your framework accordingly.
- **Design for flexibility:** Build systems that can evolve as customer expectations, technology, and market trends change.

- **Incorporate feedback:** Regularly gather insights from both customers and employees to refine and enhance service strategies.

- **Commit to continuous improvement:** Schedule routine reviews to keep the framework relevant and effective.

Following these principles ensures businesses don't just meet customer expectations—they stay ahead of them. Deloitte's CX model emphasizes operational agility and customer-driven transformation (Luck, 2024). Tools like CustomerGauge's CXM Model also help businesses track framework performance, measure improvements, and optimize for long-term customer satisfaction.

With a well-designed, customizable service framework, businesses can stop playing catch-up and start setting the pace—consistently delivering experiences that keep customers coming back.

Implementing Consistency Across Channels

Customers don't think in terms of "channels"—they just expect good service, no matter how they reach out. Whether they send a quick message on social media, hop on a live chat, or pick up the phone, they want the same level of attention, accuracy, and care. The challenge for businesses is making sure that actually happens. Without a solid strategy, service can feel scattered, leading to mixed messages, frustration, and a drop in customer trust.

Creating a Unified Messaging Strategy

One of the biggest roadblocks to consistent service is fragmented communication. If the social media team is saying one thing, the call center is saying another, and the website says something entirely different, customers are left confused—and frustrated. That's why a unified messaging strategy is so important.

This means integrating all customer touchpoints—email, phone, live chat, social media—so that no matter how someone reaches out, they get the same clear, accurate information. It also ensures that customer interactions feel seamless. A person shouldn't have to start from scratch every time they switch from one channel to another. Unified messaging helps prevent service gaps, mixed signals, and unnecessary friction (*10 Best Customer Service Strategies for Unmatched Satisfaction*, 2025).

Training Teams for Cross-Channel Excellence

Just as businesses need a unified approach, employees need to be equipped to handle different customer touchpoints. A great email response won't mean much if the phone team delivers a totally different answer. That's where cross-channel training comes in.

Employees should feel just as comfortable answering a detailed inquiry over email as they do responding to a customer's quick question on Twitter. Training should focus on adapting the message to fit each platform while keeping the core information the same. This not only builds confidence among employees but also ensures customers get a consistent experience—no matter where the conversation happens.

Making Knowledge Accessible With Shared Resources

A major reason customers get inconsistent answers? Employees don't always have access to the same information. One rep might be working off an outdated policy document, while another relies on personal experience. The fix? A centralized knowledge base.

Think of it as the single source of truth—a place where employees can find updated policies, troubleshooting steps, FAQs, and service guidelines. When teams are all pulling from the same playbook, it eliminates guesswork, speeds up response times, and prevents conflicting information (*Freshchat: Customer Messaging, Live Chat & Chatbots | Freshworks*, 2025). Plus, it helps new employees get up to speed faster, making training more efficient.

Using Monitoring and Feedback to Fine-Tune Service

Even with a strong foundation, maintaining consistency is an ongoing effort. That's where monitoring and feedback systems come in. Businesses need to regularly check in on how service is being delivered across different channels. Are response times slower in certain areas? Are customers getting conflicting information? Are there gaps in training?

Monitoring interactions helps spot these issues early so they can be corrected before they become bigger problems. And customer feedback? That's pure gold. Surveys, reviews, and direct feedback can reveal blind spots and highlight areas where service might be falling short. The key is not just collecting feedback—but actually acting on it.

Keeping Consistency an Ongoing Priority

Ensuring uniform service across all channels requires regular check-ins, ongoing training, and a commitment to making adjustments as needed. Businesses that prioritize consistency build stronger relationships with their customers because they deliver the same reliable experience, time and time again.

By integrating messaging, training teams across platforms, making knowledge easily accessible, and fine-tuning service based on real-time insights, companies can eliminate the confusion and frustration that comes from inconsistency. And when customers know they can count on a business to get it right—no matter how they reach out—those are points for trust and loyalty.

Maintaining Flexibility in Evolving Scenarios

As customer expectations shift and technology advances, businesses that build flexibility into their service frameworks stay ahead of the game. Adaptability isn't just a competitive advantage; it's essential for delivering consistently great service in an unpredictable world.

Scenario Planning

One of the best ways to stay ahead is scenario planning—anticipating potential shifts and preparing solutions before they become urgent problems. Instead of reacting to disruptions, businesses that think ahead can lead the change.

For example, imagine a game-changing technology that suddenly reshapes how customers interact with services. Companies that have already mapped out how to integrate new tools into their existing workflows won't be scrambling to catch up. This kind of proactive thinking helps businesses maintain smooth operations while keeping customers happy. Organizations that make scenario planning a regular habit aren't just resilient; they set the pace for the industry.

Encouraging Innovation

A culture of adaptability starts with innovation. When employees feel empowered to challenge the status quo and propose fresh ideas, businesses discover better, more creative ways to serve customers. Companies like Amazon continuously refine their service approach by leveraging AI and automation to enhance user experiences—proving that when innovation is baked into the culture, service excellence follows.

Encouraging experimentation doesn't just improve service; it also boosts employee morale. When teams see their ideas put into action, they stay engaged and invested in the company's success. Innovation-driven workplaces attract top talent and keep teams motivated to push boundaries and improve customer interactions.

Using Feedback Loops

Listening to customers in real-time is crucial for adaptability. Feedback loops—whether through surveys, AI-driven analytics, or direct customer interactions—help businesses identify emerging patterns and adjust accordingly.

For example, if data reveals that customers are struggling with a particular support channel, companies can act immediately rather than waiting for complaints to pile up. Responsive businesses don't just collect feedback; they turn it into action, refining their strategies to meet customer needs as they evolve.

Offering Flexible Solutions

Customers expect service on their own terms. A one-size-fits-all approach doesn't work when preferences vary widely. Providing multiple communication options—phone, chat, email, social media—gives customers control over how they engage with a brand.

Beyond just communication, businesses that embrace diverse problem-solving approaches create more inclusive and effective service frameworks. Understanding cultural nuances, technological preferences, and industry-specific needs helps companies design experiences that resonate with a broad customer base. Today's customers want personalized interactions, and flexibility ensures they get exactly that.

Leadership, Learning, and Empowerment

Building adaptability into a service framework is more than just about tools and strategies—it's a mindset that starts at the top. Leaders set the tone by fostering open-mindedness, continuous learning, and cross-team collaboration.

Investing in ongoing education, whether through workshops, online courses, or mentorship programs, ensures employees stay ahead of industry trends. The best companies don't just react to change—they train their teams to embrace it. Setting measurable goals for learning initiatives ensures that education translates into real-world service improvements.

Finally, adaptability thrives in environments where employees have the autonomy to make decisions. Trusting service teams to take the initiative encourages quick problem-solving and innovation at the front lines. Employees who feel empowered to act are more engaged, more proactive, and better equipped to meet customer needs in real-time.

Adaptability isn't a bonus—it's a necessity. Businesses that plan for change encourage innovation, listen to feedback, offer flexible solutions, and empower employees to create customer service frameworks that stand the test of time. With the right mindset and strategies, organizations can navigate shifts with confidence, keeping customers happy and operations running smoothly no matter what the future holds.

Conclusion

So, what's the big takeaway from all this? Building a customer service framework is about creating a system that helps your team shine and keeps your customers happy. Start with clear goals and standardized processes to make sure every interaction hits the mark. Use performance metrics to track how things are going and spot where you can do even better. This kind of ongoing check-in keeps your team sharp and ready for whatever comes their way.

But here's the thing: no two businesses are the same, and neither are their customers. That's why flexibility is key. By tailoring your framework to fit your unique needs, you can handle customer requests with ease and efficiency. And don't forget to listen—feedback from both customers and employees is like gold. It helps you fine-tune your approach and deliver experiences that truly stand out.

Of course, none of this works without a well-trained team. When your people have the skills and confidence to handle any situation, consistency becomes second nature. Put it all together, and you've got a framework that not only delivers great service but also builds trust and loyalty. And in the end, that's what keeps customers coming back.

Now that we've got a solid framework in place, it's time to talk about how to measure success. After all, how do you know if your strategies are working if you're not keeping track? In the next chapter, we'll learn the tools and techniques for measuring and analyzing customer satisfaction—so you can turn feedback into action and keep improving.

Chapter 7: Measuring and Analyzing Customer Satisfaction

We've discussed communication skills and the components of a successful business, but what about customer satisfaction? The first point to understand is you can't just assume your customers are happy. You've got to measure it, analyze it, and use that information to make things better. Think of it like this: if you're running a restaurant, you wouldn't just guess what dishes people like, right? You'd ask them, take notes, and tweak the menu based on their feedback. The same goes for customer service. Measuring satisfaction is how you figure out what's working, what's not, and where you can level up.

In this chapter, we're going to break it all down. We'll talk about the key metrics that matter—like Net Promoter Score (NPS) and Customer Satisfaction Score (CSAT), which we mentioned in previous chapters—and how they can give you a clear picture of how your customers feel. You'll also learn how to gather feedback in creative ways, like using social media and CRM systems, so you can hear what your customers are really saying. By the end, you'll have everything you need to measure, analyze, and improve customer satisfaction in your business. Ready to get started?

Identifying Key Metrics for Customer Satisfaction

Customer satisfaction is the driving force behind customer loyalty, brand connection, and long-term success. Tracking key metrics helps businesses understand their customers better, refine their services, and strengthen relationships. Let's break down the basic metrics that shed light on customer sentiment and expectations.

Net Promoter Score (NPS): Measuring Loyalty

Net Promoter Score (NPS) is a go-to metric for measuring customer loyalty. It's as simple as asking, "How likely are you to recommend our company to a friend or colleague?" Customers respond on a scale from 0 to 10, where scores of 9 and 10—referred to as "Promoters"—are your brand champions, while those scoring between 0 and 6—known as "Detractors"—may be unhappy or disengaged.The gap between these two groups determines your overall NPS, providing a quick read on brand perception (Raileanu, 2018).

What makes NPS so useful is that it doesn't just capture satisfaction—it helps predict future customer behavior. Tracking NPS over time lets businesses spot trends, group customers based on their responses, and take action to turn Detractors into Promoters. Companies that consistently use NPS insights to adjust their strategies often see stronger retention rates and better word-of-mouth marketing.

Customer Satisfaction Score (CSAT): Tracking Immediate Reactions

While NPS offers a broad view of customer loyalty, the Customer Satisfaction Score (CSAT) zooms in on individual experiences. After a purchase or a support call, customers are asked to rate their satisfaction on a scale, typically from 1 to 5. This quick pulse check provides real-time feedback on what's working and what needs improvement (Paryvai, 2024).

For customer service teams, CSAT is like a built-in radar for spotting trouble spots. If low scores start stacking up after support interactions, it's a clear sign something needs fixing—whether that's better training, streamlined processes, or clearer communication. CSAT helps businesses zero in on the moments that matter most, ensuring that every interaction leaves a positive impression.

Customer Effort Score (CES): Reducing Friction in Service

The Customer Effort Score (CES) is all about simplicity—how easy is it for customers to get what they need, whether that's resolving a problem, placing an order, or tracking down information? CES surveys usually phrase it like this: "The company made it easy for me to handle my issue," with customers responding on a scale from "Strongly Agree" to "Strongly Disagree."

If CES scores are high, that's a red flag. It means customers are running into roadblocks, whether it's a clunky checkout process, long support wait times, or confusing self-service options. The good news? Identifying these sticking points gives businesses a chance to streamline their processes, making life easier for customers. Research backs this up—reducing effort isn't just nice to have, it directly boosts customer loyalty since people are far more likely to stick around when things run smoothly (Raileanu, 2018).

Churn Rate: Understanding Customer Retention

Churn Rate tracks how many customers stop using a service within a set period. A rising churn rate often points to deeper issues—whether it's lackluster service, unmet expectations, or competitors luring customers away. Keeping an eye on churn patterns helps businesses figure out why customers leave and what they can do to keep them around (Paryvai, 2024).

Say a price hike leads to an uptick in cancellations—that's a sign to reassess pricing or add perks to make the cost worthwhile. If customers are bailing due to long support wait times, maybe it's time to invest in better automation or more support staff. The sooner businesses pinpoint the problem, the faster they can fix it before it starts cutting into revenue.

Each metric plays a different role in shaping customer experience strategies. NPS gauges loyalty, CSAT captures immediate feedback, CES flags service hurdles, and Churn Rate reveals retention struggles. Together, they give businesses a well-rounded picture of customer satisfaction, making it easier to refine their approach and keep customers engaged.

For businesses big and small, using these insights wisely can make a real difference. Companies that stay on top of customer feedback don't just meet expectations—they surpass them, building stronger relationships, driving revenue, and securing long-term success.

Tools for Gathering and Analyzing Feedback

When it comes to customer satisfaction, knowing what your customers think is half the battle. The good news? There are plenty of tools out there designed to help businesses collect and analyze feedback. These tools offer a roadmap for improving services, refining products, and strengthening customer relationships. Let's take a closer look at some of the most effective ways to gather and make sense of customer feedback.

Surveys and Questionnaires: Asking the Right Questions

Surveys and questionnaires are classic for a reason—they work. They let businesses go straight to the source, asking customers about their experiences, preferences, and suggestions. Whether sent via email, embedded on a website, or posted on social media, surveys can be customized to focus on specific areas. A restaurant might ask about food quality, while a software company could check in on usability. The key is crafting questions that are clear, unbiased, and designed to yield genuinely useful insights (Gherca, 2024). Well-structured surveys help businesses pinpoint exactly where they're hitting the mark and where they need to step up.

Feedback Forms: Capturing Real-Time Reactions

Feedback forms work best when they're given to customers right after an interaction while the experience is still fresh. That's why you'll often see them pop up after a hotel stay, a customer service call, or an online purchase. They provide immediate insights that help businesses address concerns before they turn into bigger problems. For example, if a hotel guest notes that their room wasn't as clean as expected, management can take swift action before it affects future stays. Beyond fixing individual issues, feedback forms show customers that their opinions matter and that the business is committed to continuous improvement (Sharma, 2025b).

Social Media Listening: Tuning Into the Conversation

Customers talk about brands all the time—on Twitter, Facebook, Instagram, TikTok, the recently popular RedNote, and beyond. Social media listening tools help businesses keep track of those conversations, whether they're filled with praise, complaints, or general feedback. By monitoring brand mentions and trending topics, companies can stay ahead of potential issues, celebrate wins, and engage with their audience in real-time. If a product launch generates a lot of buzz, businesses can ride the wave. If complaints start piling up, they can pivot quickly to address them. But social media listening is more damage control; it helps strengthen connections and create more meaningful interactions with customers.

CRM Systems: Spotting Patterns and Trends

Customer Relationship Management (CRM) systems are like a treasure trove of customer insights. They store interactions across different channels—emails, phone calls, support tickets, and live chats—giving businesses a complete view of how customers engage with them. With CRM data analysis, businesses can identify recurring issues, spot trends, and refine their customer service approach. Let's take a common complaint: long response times. If this issue appears, it might be time to invest in additional support staff or streamline workflows. Beyond troubleshooting, CRM analysis also helps businesses anticipate customer needs, making it easier to personalize interactions and deliver standout service (Gherca, 2024).

Making Feedback Work for Your Business

The real magic happens when businesses integrate these tools into a cohesive strategy. Combining survey results, social media insights, and CRM data creates a full picture of the customer journey, making it easier to turn feedback into action. Whether it’s a small business owner choosing the right tool on a budget or a customer service manager looking to improve team performance, the key is selecting tools that align with specific goals. Keeping feedback collection simple, accessible, and well-integrated with existing systems ensures that every customer's voice contributes to meaningful improvements. The better a business listens, the stronger its customer relationships—and its long-term success—will be.

Incorporating Feedback Into Service Improvements

If you want to keep your customers happy, paying attention to their feedback helps you make smarter decisions. Feedback gives you a direct line to what's working, what's not, and where you need to step up your game. But gathering feedback is only half the battle; the real magic happens when you put it to good use.

Spotting Patterns and Prioritizing Fixes

Not all feedback is created equal. Some comments are one-offs, while others highlight major trends you can't afford to ignore. If multiple customers keep bringing up the same issue—like slow response times or a confusing checkout process—that's a flashing neon sign that something needs to change. Paying attention to these recurring themes helps you focus on the areas that matter most, ensuring that time and resources go toward improvements with the biggest impact (Wellington, 2022).

Turning Feedback Into Real Action

Customers notice when businesses take their concerns seriously. Addressing feedback is proving to customers that their input directly influences how you do business. This might mean tweaking a product feature, refining a process, or offering better tutorials to clear up confusion. Whatever the fix, the key is making meaningful changes that genuinely enhance the customer experience. When customers see their input leading to real improvements, it builds trust and keeps them coming back (Tousley, 2019).

Keeping Your Team in the Loop

One of the biggest mistakes businesses make is keeping feedback locked away in reports instead of sharing it with the people who can actually do something about it. Frontline employees—the ones interacting with customers every day—need to be part of the conversation. When teams understand what customers are saying, they can adapt, innovate, and come up with solutions that align with real needs. Plus, involving employees in the process creates a sense of shared responsibility, making them feel more invested in the company's success.

Tracking Progress and Refining Strategies

Once changes are made, it's important to track whether they're actually making a difference. Documenting what you've adjusted, why you did it, and what happened afterward helps you measure success and refine your approach over time. Keeping a record of feedback-driven improvements also provides a roadmap for future decisions and proves to both customers and stakeholders that you're committed to continuous growth.

At the end of the day, collecting customer feedback means nothing if you don't put it to use. Businesses that take it seriously improve their services and strengthen customer relationships along the way.

Using Data to Drive Strategic Decisions

In today's business world, making decisions based on data is essential. Relying on gut feelings or guesswork can only get you so far, but using hard facts and real customer insights gives businesses a serious edge. When you tap into customer satisfaction data, you're improving service while also refining your overall strategy to keep customers coming back.

Making Decisions With Confidence

One of the biggest benefits of data-driven decision-making is cutting down on uncertainty. When your choices are backed by numbers instead of hunches, you reduce the risk of costly mistakes and improve your odds of success. Big companies like Amazon and Google have this down to a science. Amazon, for example, uses detailed algorithms to track customer behavior and suggest products. That approach keeps shoppers engaged and drives sales (Stobierski, 2019).

Understanding What Customers Really Want

Digging into customer data helps businesses align their strategies with what people actually need. It's how Starbucks figures out the best spots for new locations—they use location analytics to make sure their stores are in high-demand areas. This method has helped them build a strong brand that reflects customer preferences (Linker, 2024).

Predicting What's Coming Next

Looking at past trends provides insights into future possibilities. Companies that analyze historical data can anticipate changes in the market, helping them stay ahead of the competition. Sales teams do this all the time by studying past performance to forecast demand. By predicting what customers will need next, they can stock up and adjust their strategies accordingly (Stobierski, 2019).

Setting Goals That Actually Make Sense

Using data to set measurable goals makes it easier to track progress and keep teams motivated. When employees know exactly what they're working toward—and can see how their efforts contribute to the bigger picture—they're more engaged. Google's Project Oxygen is a perfect example of this in action. By analyzing data from performance reviews, they identified key traits of great managers and then built training programs to develop those skills (Stobierski, 2019).

Making Data Work for Your Business

If you want to start making more data-driven decisions, begin by defining your goals. What do you want to achieve? Maybe you're aiming to improve customer retention by 15%. In that case, analyzing customer feedback would be a great place to start to see where improvements can be made.

Once you have a clear objective, it's time to collect high-quality data. The more accurate your data, the better your decisions will be. Sources like Google Analytics, customer surveys, and social media insights provide valuable information about customer behavior and industry trends (Linker, 2024).

Turning Data Into Action

Numbers alone don't tell the full story—you need to make sense of them. Visualizing data through graphs, dashboards, and reports makes it easier to spot patterns and trends. When key insights are easy to understand, decision-makers can focus on taking action instead of sifting through spreadsheets.

And once changes are in motion, measuring their impact is the logical next step. Checking in regularly to see if adjustments are working helps businesses refine their approach over time. A strategy that's guided by continuous learning and adaptation is far more effective than one that's set in stone.

Creating a Data-Driven Culture

For data-driven decision-making to truly work, it needs to be part of the company culture. Encouraging employees at all levels to engage with data and use it to inform their choices builds a smarter, more agile organization. When everyone understands how to interpret and apply data, businesses become more proactive and prepared for whatever comes next.

For entrepreneurs, small business owners, and customer service managers, embracing data in strategic decision-making offers a powerful advantage. It helps improve customer satisfaction, strengthen customer relationships, and create a solid foundation for long-term growth. Keeping data at the core of business decisions ensures that every move is backed by insight, setting the stage for lasting success.

Conclusion

The message I want to convey in this chapter is that customer satisfaction is more than just a number. By using tools like NPS, CSAT, and CES, you can get a clear picture of how your customers feel and where you can improve. And by turning feedback into action, you'll show your customers that their opinions matter.

For managers, entrepreneurs, and business owners, this is your chance to take your service to the next level. Whether it's through surveys, social media, or CRM analysis, there are endless ways to listen to your customers and make meaningful changes. And when you do, you'll not only keep your customers happy—you'll keep them coming back.

Now that you've got a handle on measuring satisfaction, it's time to talk about what happens when things don't go as planned. In the next chapter, we'll explore how to handle difficult customers and turn challenging situations into opportunities to shine.

Chapter 8: Handling Difficult Customers and Situations

Dealing with difficult customers is part of the job when you're in customer service. Whether it's an angry client yelling over the phone or a confused customer who can't seem to make up their mind, these situations can test even the most patient professionals. But here's the thing: we should look at these moments as opportunities rather than challenges. Opportunities to show your skills, build trust, and turn a potentially negative experience into a positive one. The key is to approach these interactions with empathy, patience, and a clear strategy.

In this chapter, we'll explore how to handle tough customer interactions like a pro. We'll talk about identifying different types of difficult customers—from the aggressive to the indecisive—and how to tailor your approach to each one. You'll learn how to de-escalate tense situations, build resilience, and even turn negative experiences into opportunities for growth. By the end, you'll have a toolkit of strategies to handle any customer situation with confidence and professionalism.

Identifying Types of Challenging Interactions

Difficult customers are part of the game in any business, and knowing how to handle them starts with recognizing the different types you'll encounter. Some customers are aggressive and confrontational, others are confused and just need some guidance. Then there are the indecisive ones who can't quite make up their minds, the impatient ones who expect lightning-fast service, and the know-it-alls who think they have all the answers. Figuring out who you're dealing with makes it much easier to adjust your approach and keep the interaction productive.

Handling Aggressive Customers

Aggressive customers tend to come in hot, raising their voices, using harsh language, or even demanding immediate action. Their frustration usually comes from feeling unheard or having unmet expectations. The best way to handle them? Stay calm. Matching their energy with defensiveness or irritation will only escalate things. Instead, acknowledge their frustration and reassure them that you're there to help. Something as simple as, "I can see why that's frustrating. Let's work together to fix it," can go a long way in diffusing tension. When customers feel heard, they're more likely to shift from combative to cooperative.

Helping Confused Customers

Some customers are overwhelmed by too much information or simply don't understand how a product or service works. They'll often ask the same question multiple times or seem unsure about what they need. These customers require patience and clear, step-by-step explanations. Instead of bombarding them with technical details, simplify things with relatable examples or analogies. If they seem hesitant, offering reassurance and guiding them through their options can help them feel more confident in their decisions. The goal is to make them feel supported rather than embarrassed for not knowing something.

Guiding Indecisive Customers

Indecisive customers can be tough because they struggle to make a choice—even when all the options are laid out. They might be afraid of making the wrong decision, overwhelmed by too many choices, or simply unsure of what they really want. The key to helping them is to ask the right questions and figure out what's holding them back. Are they worried about the price? Do they need reassurance about quality? Once you pinpoint their hesitation, you can offer targeted recommendations or incentives like discounts or guarantees to help them commit. Sometimes, creating a sense of urgency—without pressuring them too much—can also push them toward a decision.

Managing Impatient Customers

We've all dealt with customers who expect instant results. They tap their fingers, sigh loudly, or repeatedly ask how much longer something will take. The trick with impatient customers is to manage expectations early. If there's going to be a delay, let them know upfront. Regular updates can also help—keeping them informed reassures them that they haven't been forgotten. Quick responses and a proactive approach make a big difference in turning an impatient customer into a satisfied one.

Engaging With Know-It-All Customers

Some customers love to prove they know more than you do, whether it's about the product, the policies, or even how to run the business. The worst thing you can do? Argue with them. Instead, acknowledge their knowledge and steer the conversation in a collaborative direction. "That's a great point! Here's another way to look at it..." or "You seem really familiar with this—let me add something you might find useful." When you respect their expertise instead of challenging it, they're more likely to engage positively instead of turning the conversation into a battle.

Recognizing these different customer types isn't just about labeling people—it's about understanding their motivations and responding in a way that keeps things from escalating. When employees know what to expect and how to handle each situation, they're more confident and prepared. Training programs that include role-playing different customer scenarios can be a turning point, helping teams build the skills needed to navigate even the toughest interactions.

Handling difficult customers is all about adaptability. The more you fine-tune your approach based on who you're dealing with, the better the outcome for everyone involved. And who knows? A tough customer today might just turn into a loyal one tomorrow with the right handling.

Strategies for De-escalating Tense Situations

Dealing with upset customers isn't easy, but with the right approach, you can turn a heated situation into a productive conversation. The key? Knowing how to bring the tension down instead of letting it spiral out of control. A few smart strategies—starting with active listening—can make all the difference.

Active Listening: More Than Just Nodding Along

When a frustrated customer comes at you with complaints, it's tempting to jump straight into problem-solving mode. But before offering solutions, they need to feel heard. That's where active listening comes in. It's not just about hearing the words—it's about understanding the emotions behind them.

For example, if a customer is upset about a service delay, responding with something like, "I hear you. It sounds like this delay has been really frustrating, and I completely understand why that would be upsetting," validates their feelings. It shows them you're not just waiting for your turn to talk—you actually care (Waite, 2024). And once they feel acknowledged, they're much more likely to work with you toward a solution.

The Power of Empathy Statements

Empathy is one of the best tools in your customer service toolkit. A simple "I can see how this would be frustrating" or "That sounds really stressful, and I want to help" can instantly lower defenses. People want to know they're not just another number in a queue—they want to feel understood (M, 2025). Even if you can't fix the issue immediately, showing that you genuinely care goes a long way in calming emotions and earning trust.

Keeping Your Cool (Even When They Don't)

Nothing escalates a tense situation faster than matching a customer's frustration with your own. Staying calm—even when they're anything but—helps set the tone for the entire conversation.

Simple techniques like taking a deep breath before responding or keeping your voice steady can stop an interaction from spiraling. A calm demeanor signals to the customer that the situation is under control, which can help them relax, too (Waite, 2024). It's a classic case of "lead by example"—if you stay composed, chances are they'll follow suit.

Setting Boundaries Without Losing Professionalism

While de-escalation is the goal, there are times when a line needs to be drawn. If a customer becomes aggressive or starts using abusive language, it's okay to set boundaries. A polite but firm statement like, "I want to help resolve this, but I need us to keep the conversation respectful," sends a clear message: you're here to help, but you won't tolerate hostility.

Boundaries protect both you and the customer by ensuring that conversations stay productive. Plus, when handled tactfully, they reinforce a professional environment where real solutions can be found.

Spotting Patterns to Prevent Future Issues

Recognizing common complaints isn't just about handling today's problems—it's about preventing them in the future. If the same issues keep coming up, it's a sign that something bigger needs fixing. When businesses take the time to analyze recurring problems, they can adjust their approach, reducing frustration for both customers and employees (Waite, 2024).

Asking the Right Questions

Open-ended questions are a great way to get to the heart of a problem. Instead of assuming you know what's wrong, ask something like, "Can you walk me through what happened?" or "What would be the ideal outcome for you?" These kinds of questions encourage customers to share details that might help you solve the issue more effectively (M, 2025).

When people feel like their voice matters, they're more likely to work with you toward a resolution rather than against you.

Positive Language: Framing Solutions Instead of Problems

Words matter a lot. Instead of saying, "There's nothing we can do," try "Here's what we can do to fix this." That small shift in wording changes the entire tone of the conversation, keeping things solution-focused instead of shutting the customer down (M, 2025).

Positive language reassures customers that you're on their side, which makes them more willing to collaborate instead of just venting their frustrations.

Owning Mistakes and Making Things Right

Sometimes, a simple apology is the most effective de-escalation tool. If your company made a mistake, acknowledge it. Saying, "I'm really sorry for the inconvenience. Here's what we can do to make it right," shows accountability and reassures the customer that their concerns matter.

Offering a small compensation—like a discount or a replacement—can go a long way in turning a bad experience into a positive one. Customers appreciate when businesses take responsibility and genuinely try to fix things. In many cases, a well-handled mistake can actually increase customer loyalty.

By focusing on active listening, empathy, composure, and smart communication, you can turn difficult customer interactions into opportunities. These strategies defuse tension in the moment while building long-term trust and loyalty. That's what great customer service is all about.

Building Resilience in Customer-Facing Roles

A fact: Working in customer service can be tough. Some days, you're juggling five conversations at once, dealing with frustrated customers, and trying to keep a smile on your face. That's where resilience comes in. But resilience isn't toughing it out; it's bouncing back after tough interactions, staying motivated, and keeping your cool no matter what gets thrown your way.

Managing Stress Effectively

A big part of resilience is learning how to manage stress. One of the best ways to do this is through mindfulness techniques—things like deep breathing, guided meditation, or even just taking a moment to reset before your next interaction. Studies have shown that mindfulness can help service reps stay focused, patient, and calm under pressure. Another great stress-buster? Movement. Whether it's a quick walk on your break or some simple stretches, physical activity can help clear your mind and boost your energy.

Building a Strong Support System

Resilience thrives in a supportive environment. Having a strong peer support system can make all the difference. Team check-ins, casual debriefs after a tough shift, or even just knowing you have colleagues who understand what you're going through can help lighten the emotional load. Companies that encourage open discussions about workplace challenges create teams that are stronger, more connected, and better equipped to handle stress.

Embracing a Growth Mindset

Another key to resilience? A growth mindset. This means seeing challenges as learning opportunities rather than setbacks. When something goes wrong—say, a customer lashes out unfairly—it's easy to take it personally. But by shifting your perspective and asking, "What can I learn from this?" you turn difficult experiences into chances to improve. Many companies invest in workshops that help employees reframe challenges positively. In these sessions, team members share stories of setbacks that led to valuable lessons, reinforcing the idea that every tough interaction is a chance to grow.

Learning from Real-World Resilience Programs

Some companies have already made resilience training a core part of their employee development. For example, Nipro rolled out an eight-session resilience program focused on emotional intelligence and stress management (Gupta, 2023). Google also offers a resilience podcast featuring expert insights on handling workplace stress (Gupta, 2023). These programs highlight how organizations can actively support their employees' well-being and professional growth.

Prioritizing Self-Care

Beyond structured training, simple every day habits can make a big difference. Getting enough sleep, eating balanced meals, and setting boundaries around workload can all help prevent burnout. Prioritizing self-care isn't just a nice to have—it's essential for maintaining energy and focus in a high-stress environment.

Implementing Workplace Wellness Initiatives

Many companies have also started implementing wellness programs that focus on mental, physical, and emotional health. From fitness classes and yoga sessions to stress-relief activities like art therapy, these initiatives promote a more balanced, resilient workforce. Siemens Healthineers, for example, introduced an online resilience training program during the COVID-19 pandemic, offering meditation and breathing exercises to help employees stay grounded (Gupta, 2023).

Encouraging Peer-Led Initiatives

Another great strategy? Peer-led initiatives. Employees who have developed strong resilience skills can lead workshops or group discussions, sharing their own experiences and strategies. These peer-led sessions create a supportive, relatable learning environment where team members feel comfortable sharing and growing together.

In summary, resilience is learning how to navigate stress effectively. By focusing on stress management, peer support, a growth mindset, and practical self-care strategies, customer service professionals can build the mental and emotional strength they need to handle anything that comes their way.

Converting Negative Experiences Into Positive Outcomes

Unhappy customers are part of the job. The good news is that every negative interaction is a chance to turn things around. Instead of seeing complaints as just another headache, think of them as opportunities to improve and even build stronger customer relationships. When handled well, a bad experience can turn a frustrated customer into one of your biggest advocates.

Finding the Lesson in the Complaint

No one likes getting complaints, but they can actually be a goldmine of useful information. Patterns in customer feedback often highlight deeper issues that need fixing. Say multiple customers are confused about your billing process—that's a clear sign it might need simplification or better communication. Taking these lessons to heart and making proactive changes can prevent future frustrations and create a smoother experience for everyone.

Turning Complaints Into Collaboration

Customers want to feel heard, and one of the best ways to show them they matter is by involving them in solutions. Asking for feedback—whether through surveys, follow-up emails, or casual conversations—signals that you value their opinions. During my time working at a marina, I learned how to handle difficult customers while building long-lasting relationships. One of the toughest parts of the job was enforcing policies like chaining boats to the dock after 60 days of non-payment of dockage dues. It was an embarrassing moment for the boat owner, but it was necessary to protect the business.

Once the dues were paid, we'd unchain the boat, and I always made sure to approach the situation with empathy and understanding. Over time, I got to know 99% of the 1,200 boat slips by name—not just the owners but their pets and family members, too. This personal touch created a positive environment where customers felt valued, even when tough policies had to be enforced.

Unfortunately, after the company was sold, things changed rapidly. The individual customer service and empathy disappeared, and everyone was treated as a number or a dollar sign. This shift highlighted how critical personal connections and empathy are in customer service. Even in difficult situations, treating customers with respect and understanding can turn potential conflicts into opportunities to build trust and loyalty.

The Power of a Thoughtful Follow-Up

Following up after resolving an issue to make sure the customer is satisfied brings great benefits. A sincere apology paired with real action can go a long way in rebuilding trust. Sending a personalized message or checking in after a resolution shows that the company genuinely cares. Research suggests that businesses that engage with customers after resolving an issue are more likely to retain loyalty and even gain positive word-of-mouth referrals (Pratt, 2024). A simple “We appreciate your feedback and hope you’re happy with the solution” can make a big difference.

Celebrating Success Stories

Nothing reinforces a customer-first culture better than sharing real stories of positive change. When a complaint leads to a meaningful improvement, make sure to highlight it. Internally, these stories can boost team morale by showing that their efforts truly make an impact. Externally, showcasing success stories on your website or social media proves to customers that you listen, learn, and take action. For instance, if a travel company implements a real-time notification system after customer feedback about flight delays, sharing that story publicly helps build credibility and trust.

Turning Customers Into Advocates

Great service extends to ongoing engagement. Customers who feel valued and respected often become vocal supporters of the brand. Encouraging happy customers to share their experiences through testimonials, reviews, or even social media shout-outs helps reinforce a positive brand reputation. Hosting Q and A sessions or featuring customer stories in marketing campaigns can further build community and loyalty.

Going the Extra Mile

Sometimes, it's the little things that make the biggest impact. A heartfelt apology is great, but adding an extra touch—like a discount, a small gift, or priority service—can leave a lasting impression. At the marina, I found that simply taking the time to listen to customers and show genuine care—like remembering their names, their pets, and their stories—went a long way in building loyalty. Even when enforcing tough policies, like chaining a boat for non-payment, I made sure to handle the situation with empathy and respect.

These small gestures, combined with consistent personal connections, turned potentially negative experiences into opportunities to strengthen relationships. Customers appreciated being treated as individuals, not just numbers, and many remained loyal even after the company changed hands.

Conclusion

Handling tough customer interactions isn't easy, but it's a skill that can be mastered with the right mindset and strategies. In this chapter, we've broken down the different types of difficult customers and explored ways to navigate each situation effectively. Whether it's keeping your cool with an angry customer or guiding a confused one toward the right solution, every interaction is a chance to build trust and strengthen relationships.

Understanding why customers behave the way they do is *mandatory* in today's business ecosystem. When you approach problems with empathy and curiosity instead of frustration, you're more likely to find solutions that work for everyone. We've covered key techniques like active listening, using empathy statements, and maintaining composure—all of which help to turn tense moments into productive conversations.

Beyond the customer, we also looked at what it takes to build resilience in service roles. Stress is part of the job, but with solid stress management techniques and a strong support system, it doesn't have to be overwhelming. The more you recognize patterns in customer concerns and use them to improve your processes, the better equipped you'll be to handle future challenges.

In customer service, knowing how to handle difficult situations with confidence makes the difference.

When businesses commit to learning from each interaction, prioritizing communication, and supporting their teams, they create an environment where both employees and customers feel valued. And that's the foundation of long-term success and loyalty.

Chapter 9: Cultivating a Customer-Centric Culture

Let's talk about what it really means to put customers at the heart of your organization. It's not just about saying the right things or rolling out a new policy; it's about creating a culture where every decision, every action, and every interaction revolves around the customer. Think of it as a mindset that everyone, from the CEO to the newest hire, adopts. More than a strategy, it's a way of doing business that makes customers feel valued, heard, and appreciated.

This chapter is all about how to build that kind of culture. We'll explore how to craft a vision that inspires your team, align your mission with customer needs, and create systems that keep everyone focused on delivering exceptional service. Along the way, you'll see how real-world companies have made this shift and the impact it's had on their success.

When you get to "Conclusion," you'll have the tools to transform your organization into one where customer focus becomes a way of life.

Defining a Customer-Centric Organizational Vision

Creating a customer-centric culture starts with a clear vision—one that puts customers at the heart of everything the company does. Think of it as the organization's north star, guiding every decision, action, and interaction. But having a vision isn't just about writing a catchy statement and calling it a day. It has to be something that truly resonates, something that employees actually believe in. A strong vision statement sets the tone, aligns teams, and reinforces the company's dedication to delivering outstanding customer experiences.

Crafting a Vision That Inspires

A well-crafted vision is about embedding customer commitment into the company's DNA. It should be simple, powerful, and easy to remember. When every employee, from frontline staff to top executives, knows exactly what the organization stands for, they can actively contribute to making it a reality. A vision statement that's consistently communicated and reinforced ensures that customer satisfaction becomes a mindset that drives the entire organization (*Building a Customer Experience Vision*, n.d.).

Aligning Vision and Mission

Of course, a vision alone isn't enough. That's where the company's mission comes in. If the vision is the destination, the mission is the roadmap. A strong mission statement breaks the vision down into tangible actions, helping employees understand how their daily work contributes to the bigger picture. It's about more than just words—it's about defining clear, actionable goals that inspire employees to take ownership of their role in delivering exceptional service. When customer service excellence is woven into the mission, employees feel a stronger connection to their work, knowing their efforts have a real impact.

Engaging Stakeholders in the Vision

To make this vision truly meaningful, it's crucial to get stakeholders involved in the process. That includes employees, customers, and even business partners. When people feel like they've had a say in shaping the vision, they're far more likely to support and embody it. Bringing in different perspectives also ensures that the vision reflects real-world customer needs rather than just leadership's best guess. Simple steps like employee brainstorming sessions, customer surveys, and stakeholder discussions can help refine the vision and make it something everyone can rally behind.

Keeping the Vision Relevant

Customer expectations change, and so should your vision. A vision that stays stagnant quickly becomes outdated. That's why businesses need to keep it fresh by regularly checking in and making adjustments based on feedback. Are customers asking for faster service? More personalized interactions? A better digital experience? Listening to this feedback and making tweaks shows that the company is serious about evolving with its customers. Reviewing the vision every year or two ensures it stays relevant and keeps employees aligned with the latest expectations.

Take a retail company, for example. Maybe their original vision focused on providing highly personalized in-store experiences. But as online shopping took off, customer feedback started pointing toward a need for a more seamless digital experience. By adjusting the vision to include top-tier digital interactions—without losing the personal touch—they stay relevant while maintaining their core values. This kind of adaptability strengthens customer trust and loyalty over time.

Embedding the Vision Into Company Culture

Companies should embed customer-focused values into their culture from day one, making sure employees understand why it matters. Training programs, internal communication, and leadership reinforcement all play a role in keeping the vision alive. Employees should feel empowered to make decisions that align with customer needs, knowing they're supported in delivering great experiences.

Ensuring Accountability and Measuring Success

And finally, accountability is key. It's one thing to set a vision, but it's another to make sure it actually drives results. Organizations should put systems in place to track progress, whether that's through customer satisfaction scores, employee feedback, or other performance metrics. Encouraging collaboration between departments helps ensure that customer service excellence is a shared responsibility across the entire company.

A customer-centric vision is what separates great companies from the rest. When done right, it unites teams, strengthens customer relationships, and lays the foundation for long-term success.

Building Team Dynamics Centered on Service Excellence

Creating a customer-centric culture involves building a team that genuinely cares about delivering great service. A strong, cohesive team that thrives on collaboration and shared purpose is the foundation of service excellence. But great teams don't happen by accident. It takes intentional effort, thoughtful training, and a culture that celebrates teamwork and outstanding service.

Training That Goes Beyond the Basics

Let's start with training. A good training program gives employees the confidence and skills to handle any customer interaction with ease. That means covering both technical know-how and the soft skills that turn a routine transaction into a memorable experience. Sure, employees need to understand the products or services they're representing, but just as important is their ability to listen actively, show empathy, and problem-solve on the fly.

One of the best ways to reinforce these skills is through role-playing exercises. Practicing real-world scenarios helps employees get comfortable with handling difficult situations before they happen in the wild. The key is to keep training fresh—regular updates based on customer feedback and evolving market trends ensure that employees stay ahead of the game (Wilson, 2023).

Strengthening Bonds Through Team-Building

Beyond training, team-building activities are essential for creating a workplace where employees feel connected and supported. When people trust and respect their coworkers, collaboration becomes second nature. The best part? Team-building doesn't have to mean awkward icebreakers or trust falls (unless you're into that). Instead, it can be as simple as team lunches, problem-solving workshops, or even group volunteer opportunities.

The goal is to break down barriers between roles and departments, creating an environment where knowledge-sharing and support are the norms. When teams feel like they're in it together, they're more likely to go the extra mile for customers—and for each other.

Keeping the Conversation Going With Service Excellence Meetings

Regular team meetings focused on service excellence help keep customer satisfaction at the forefront. These meetings are a chance to share success stories, tackle challenges, and brainstorm ways to improve. The key is making them engaging, not just another obligatory meeting on the calendar.

Celebrating wins—big or small—motivates employees and reinforces what great service looks like. At the same time, discussing challenges in a collaborative setting promotes problem-solving and innovation. Encouraging participation from employees at all levels ensures fresh perspectives and ideas that can lead to meaningful improvements.

Encouraging Cross-Departmental Collaboration

In today's business world, where customer experience can make or break a company, teamwork across departments is a matter of *life or death*. When different teams work together seamlessly, they create a unified, hassle-free experience that keeps customers happy and coming back. Cross-departmental collaboration builds stronger customer relationships and turns them into long-term advocates.

Breaking Down Silos With Interdepartmental Workshops

One of the best ways to foster collaboration is by bringing people together—literally. Interdepartmental workshops create a space where employees from different teams can discuss challenges, share insights, and work on solutions together. These sessions help break down the silos that often prevent smooth communication and teamwork.

For example, imagine a workshop where sales, marketing, and customer support teams sit down to tackle common customer complaints. Marketing gains direct insight into what customers are struggling with, sales learns how to set better expectations, and support gets a clearer picture of what customers were promised. Everyone leaves with a deeper understanding of each other's roles and a shared commitment to improving the customer experience. These workshops build trust and ensure that every department is pulling in the same direction (Nicastro, 2023).

Setting Shared Goals for a Unified Vision

If different departments are chasing separate objectives, customers can feel the disconnect. That's why setting shared goals is key. When all teams work toward a common purpose—like reducing response times, improving product usability, or enhancing customer satisfaction—it ensures that every decision supports the bigger picture.

For instance, a company looking to boost its NPS could align its product development, quality assurance, and user experience teams to create a customer-driven roadmap. By incorporating real user feedback into their planning, they can tackle key pain points together. When teams see the direct impact of their combined efforts, collaboration stops feeling like extra work and starts feeling like a win-win for everyone involved.

Establishing Feedback Loops for Continuous Improvement

Open and ongoing communication is what keeps collaboration alive. Regular feedback loops allow teams to share insights, track progress, and adjust strategies based on real customer interactions. Instead of each department working in isolation, they stay informed about what's working, what's not, and how to pivot accordingly.

A great way to implement this is through monthly cross-departmental meetings where team representatives present findings from customer surveys, reviews, or direct interactions. These sessions help spread valuable insights across the organization so that no one is left in the dark. Companies like Oracle have successfully used feedback loops to refine customer-related processes, proving that when departments share knowledge, everyone benefits—including the customers. (*Maximizing Customer Experience through Interdepartmental Collaboration | Guidde*, 2023)

Celebrating Wins to Reinforce Collaboration

Nothing motivates people to keep collaborating like seeing their efforts recognized. Celebrating successes—whether it's launching a new feature that required input from multiple teams or improving customer satisfaction scores through a joint effort—reinforces the value of teamwork.

Recognition can take many forms, from formal awards to casual team lunches, but the goal is the same: to show employees that their contributions matter. Publicly acknowledging collaborative wins helps foster a culture where teamwork is valued and encouraged. When people see that working together leads to meaningful results (and maybe even a little celebration), they'll be even more motivated to collaborate in the future.

When teams work together with a shared vision, open communication, and a culture of recognition, they set the foundation for long-term success.

Recognizing and Rewarding Customer Service Excellence

If you want to build a truly customer-focused culture, recognizing and rewarding great service is essential. When employees feel valued for their efforts, they're more motivated and feel inspired to keep raising the bar. Think about it—who doesn't want to feel appreciated for going above and beyond? Recognition programs make that appreciation loud and clear, reinforcing the idea that customer service excellence isn't just expected, it's celebrated. And when employees feel valued, they bring their best to every customer interaction (Furjanic, 2024).

Making Recognition a Priority

A solid recognition program goes beyond the occasional "Great job!" in passing. It's about building a culture where outstanding service is consistently acknowledged. The best programs are simple, clear, and deeply embedded in the company's day-to-day operations. Employees should always know what behaviors and achievements will earn them recognition—and leaders should actively look for opportunities to highlight great work.

Boosting Team Motivation With Incentives

While individual recognition is important, team-based incentives can take service excellence to a whole new level. When teams have shared goals—and meaningful rewards for hitting them—it creates a natural drive to work together. Whether it's bonuses, extra time off, or even a shout-out in a company meeting, these incentives make employees feel like their efforts matter. Plus, they strengthen team dynamics, encouraging colleagues to support and learn from one another. A motivated team directly translates into better customer experiences.

Letting Customer Feedback Guide Recognition

What is the best way to measure great service? Ask the people experiencing it—your customers. Integrating customer feedback into the recognition process adds authenticity and makes employees feel even more connected to the company's mission. When employees see firsthand how their efforts impact real people, it reinforces their commitment to service. Whether it's a glowing review, a social media mention, or direct feedback from a satisfied customer, using these moments to recognize employees creates a powerful cycle of motivation and improvement (*Blog - Semos Cloud*, 2024).

Celebrating Milestones—Big and Small

Recognizing service anniversaries, major achievements, or even small wins can keep employees engaged and energized. Celebrations don't have to be elaborate—a quick mention in a team meeting, a newsletter feature, or a simple thank-you note can go a long way. What matters most is consistency. When employees know their hard work won't go unnoticed, they'll stay motivated to keep delivering outstanding service.

Making Recognition a Daily Habit

Recognition works best when it's part of the company's DNA—not just an occasional event. That's why peer recognition programs can be so effective. Encouraging employees to acknowledge each other's contributions fosters a culture where appreciation is constant, not just something that comes from leadership. When employees feel valued by both their managers and their colleagues, it strengthens team cohesion and creates a more positive workplace.

Investing in Growth as a Form of Recognition

Another powerful way to recognize employees? Invest in their future. Offering ongoing training, mentorship opportunities, or even access to new projects shows employees that their contributions matter—and that the company believes in their potential. When employees feel supported in their growth, they're more likely to stay engaged and committed to delivering great service.

Recognizing and rewarding customer service excellence builds a work environment where people genuinely want to do their best. Employees who feel appreciated are more likely to go the extra mile, handle tough situations with patience, and create meaningful connections with customers. That's the kind of culture that doesn't just boost employee morale—it strengthens customer loyalty and drives long-term success (Furjanic, 2024).

Conclusion

Building a customer-centric culture doesn't happen overnight. It takes time, effort, and commitment from everyone in the organization. But the payoff? It's huge. When customers feel valued and heard, they're more likely to stick around and recommend your business to others.

Throughout this chapter, we've explored how to create a culture that puts customers first. It starts with a clear vision—one that inspires your team and keeps everyone focused on delivering exceptional service. By involving stakeholders and regularly revisiting that vision, you ensure it stays relevant and aligned with customer needs.

We also talked about the importance of teamwork and collaboration. Training programs, team-building activities, and recognition systems all play a role in empowering employees and creating a cohesive, service-focused team. When departments work together seamlessly, customers notice—and they appreciate it.

Finally, we looked at the power of recognition. Celebrating achievements, big and small, keeps your team motivated and reinforces the importance of great service. When employees feel appreciated, they're more likely to go the extra mile for customers.

Now that you've got the foundation for a customer-centric culture, it's time to focus on keeping it fresh and relevant. In the next chapter, we'll explore how to commit to continuous improvement and adapt to the ever-changing needs of your customers.

Chapter 10: Commitment to Continuous Improvement

Let's talk about getting better—not just once in a while, but every single day. Continuous improvement is a way of thinking that keeps your business sharp, adaptable, and ready to meet whatever comes its way. It's about never settling for "good enough" and always looking for ways to raise the bar.

This chapter is all about how to make continuous improvement a part of your DNA. We'll explore how feedback loops can help you gather insights and turn them into real, actionable changes. You'll see how listening to your customers and your team can lead to happier clients, smoother processes, and a more motivated workforce.

By the end, you'll have the tools to keep your service practices fresh, relevant, and always improving. Because when you're committed to getting better every day, there's no limit to how far you can go.

Establishing a System for Continuous Feedback

If there's one thing that can make or break a company's ability to improve, it's feedback. But not just any feedback—continuous, actionable input that actually leads to change. Whether you're running a small business, leading a customer service team, or managing a growing company, having a reliable system for collecting and using feedback is key to staying ahead of customer expectations.

Creating solid feedback loops builds a culture where input is valued, acted upon, and used to drive real improvements. When customers see that their voices matter, they're more likely to stay loyal. And when employees feel heard, they become more engaged and proactive. According to Brett & Brett (2024), customer feedback—whether through surveys, direct interviews, or post-interaction reviews—can provide clear insights into what's working and what needs fixing. For instance, a customer support team might notice a recurring complaint in post-call surveys. Instead of just logging the issue, they tweak their approach, train their team differently, and suddenly, satisfaction scores start climbing. That's the power of feedback in action.

Turning Feedback Into Action

But collecting feedback is only half the equation—what really matters is what you do with it. Simply gathering input without acting on it is like having a GPS but never looking at the directions. The real impact comes from taking that data, spotting patterns, and making improvements. When employees see that their suggestions or customer insights actually lead to change, it creates a sense of ownership and pride in their work. And that engagement? It translates directly into better service and stronger team morale. Imagine a SaaS company that keeps hearing complaints about a complicated interface. By simplifying the design based on user feedback, they make customers happier and their products easier to sell and support.

Finding the Right Frequency

Timing is another big factor. Gathering feedback too often can overwhelm both customers and employees, but waiting too long can make insights outdated. Finding the right balance is key. Some businesses thrive on quarterly surveys, while others use real-time social media monitoring or customer sentiment tools to get a constant pulse on their audience. The right approach depends on the industry, the customer base, and the kind of insights you need. Brereton (2024) emphasizes that monitoring implemented changes consistently is just as important as making the changes in the first place—because if something isn't working, you need to know sooner rather than later.

Measuring the Impact of Change

And that brings us to the final step: evaluating impact. Making a change based on feedback is great, but how do you know if it actually worked? Tracking key metrics—whether it's customer satisfaction scores, retention rates, or response times—ensures that improvements are doing what they're supposed to. If a company updates its billing system after customer complaints but still gets the same frustrated feedback, it's a sign that something's still off. Regular check-ins and adjustments keep the process dynamic, ensuring that businesses don't just react to problems but actively refine their services.

Feedback as a Driver of Innovation

A strong feedback system fixes issues, but more importantly, it fuels innovation. When teams are encouraged to experiment and propose changes based on real customer insights, they start thinking ahead rather than just responding to problems. That's how businesses build a reputation for being customer-focused and forward-thinking. And the best part? Companies that consistently act on feedback don't just improve their services—they also gain a competitive edge, turning satisfied customers into vocal advocates.

Encouraging Innovation in Service Methods

Creating an environment where innovation thrives starts with encouraging creativity at all levels. This means giving employees the freedom to take risks, explore new ideas, and experiment with different approaches without the fear of failure. When teams feel empowered to think outside the box, they're more likely to develop groundbreaking service techniques that set a company apart from its competitors. Encouraging risk-taking doesn't mean embracing recklessness—it means fostering an atmosphere where learning from mistakes is just as valued as achieving success.

The Power of Recognition in Innovation

People are far more likely to contribute ideas when they know their efforts are appreciated. That's why recognition is such a powerful tool in fostering creativity. Acknowledging employees who bring forward innovative solutions—whether through verbal praise in meetings, company newsletters, or internal awards—can inspire others to follow suit. Recognition doesn't have to be extravagant; small but meaningful gestures reinforce the message that fresh thinking is not only welcomed but essential to the company's growth.

Equipping Teams With the Right Tools and Training

Creativity doesn't happen in a vacuum. Employees need access to training and resources that help them develop problem-solving skills and expand their perspectives. Workshops on creative thinking, brainstorming techniques, and cross-training initiatives expose teams to different viewpoints and methodologies. For example, a customer service manager attending a workshop on design thinking might learn new ways to redesign user experiences for better customer engagement. Investing in professional development signals to employees that the organization values their growth, ultimately encouraging continuous innovation.

Providing Space for Innovation

Dedicated innovation spaces—whether physical or digital—can make a huge difference in how teams approach problem-solving. A digital platform where employees can share and collaborate on new ideas, for instance, ensures transparency and encourages cross-departmental contributions. Such spaces create an environment where brainstorming and collaboration become part of the daily workflow rather than occasional activities. By establishing these hubs, companies ensure that innovation is embedded into their operational DNA (Dr. Henike, 2025).

Structured Evaluation of New Ideas

Innovation should be exciting, but it also needs to be strategic. Not every idea will be a winner, which is why structured evaluation processes are key. Organizations should develop clear criteria for assessing new ideas and consider pilot testing before full-scale implementation. Pilot programs allow teams to refine concepts in a low-risk setting, ensuring that only the most viable ideas move forward. For example, a small business owner looking to introduce a new customer feedback mechanism might first test a simplified version with a limited audience to gauge its effectiveness before rolling it out more broadly. This approach reduces risk while still fostering an innovation-friendly environment.

Embedding Innovation Into Everyday Operations

Companies that make innovation a daily priority often see the biggest rewards. Some organizations, like 3M, have famously allowed employees to dedicate a portion of their time to personal projects, leading to revolutionary breakthroughs (Manly et al., 2023). When employees have the opportunity to innovate as part of their regular workflow rather than as an afterthought, creativity becomes second nature. Embedding innovation into the business model ensures that companies remain adaptable, responsive, and ahead of the curve in a constantly evolving market.

Innovation as a Driver of Employee Engagement

Beyond improving products and services, fostering innovation strengthens workplace culture. Employees who feel heard and valued are more engaged and invested in their organization's success. This sense of empowerment not only enhances job satisfaction but also contributes to higher retention rates. When individuals see their creative contributions making a tangible impact, they become more motivated to contribute actively to the company's growth and evolution.

Committing to Long-Term Innovation

Encouraging creativity in service delivery requires more than occasional workshops or periodic recognition. It demands a sustained commitment to fostering a culture where innovation is a core part of the organization's identity. By making innovation a daily habit—through recognition, resources, structured evaluation, and dedicated innovation spaces—businesses position themselves to navigate today's market challenges while staying prepared for future opportunities.

The businesses that lead the way in service excellence aren't just those with the best processes today but those that continually evolve, adapt, and embrace fresh ideas for the future.

Adapting to Changing Market Trends

In business, staying ahead of the curve is a necessity. Customer expectations shift, new technologies emerge, and industry landscapes evolve at lightning speed. If a company wants to remain competitive, it needs to be flexible, proactive, and always ready to pivot. That's where market research comes in.

Market Research: Staying in the Know

Market research is like having a crystal ball—except it's backed by data rather than guesswork. Keeping an eye on consumer behavior, industry trends, and emerging tech helps businesses anticipate changes before they happen. For example, if reports show an increasing preference for eco-friendly products, companies that act fast can tap into a growing market segment while also aligning with customer values. It's not just about reacting; it's about positioning your business as a leader rather than a follower.

Flexibility in Services: The Power of Adaptability

Having flexible service protocols means your business can roll with the punches instead of scrambling when unexpected changes hit. Think of these protocols as structured guidelines with built-in adaptability. If a sudden shift—like a new social media platform taking over the market—affects how customers interact with businesses, those with flexible strategies can seamlessly adjust. A rigid approach, on the other hand, can leave a company struggling to catch up. Staying adaptable ensures a business remains resilient and consistently meets customer needs.

Keeping an Eye on Competitors: Learning From the Best (and Worst)

Competitor analysis is a game-changer. Watching what industry leaders (and struggling businesses) are doing can offer key insights into what works and what doesn't. If a rival company rolls out a customer service features that's getting rave reviews, it's worth evaluating whether a similar approach could work for your business. On the flip side, seeing a competitor stumble can highlight what to avoid. Learning from others helps businesses refine their strategies without making the same costly mistakes.

Feedback and Adjustment Cycles: Keeping It Relevant

Adapting to trends is an ongoing process. Regular feedback loops help businesses fine-tune their strategies in real time. Customer input, employee insights, and performance metrics should all factor into continuous service improvements. The key is making feedback actionable. Gathering data is one thing, but using it to drive real change is what separates stagnant companies from those that thrive.

SMART Goals: A Clear Path to Adaptation

When shifting with the market, setting SMART goals (Specific, Measurable, Achievable, Relevant, and Time-bound) is essential. Having clear objectives allows businesses to track progress, measure impact, and tweak strategies along the way. For instance, if the goal is to increase market share by 15% within a year, breaking it down into measurable milestones ensures that adjustments can be made if the strategy isn't working as expected.

Leveraging Marketing Analytics: Data-Driven Decisions

Robust analytics tools are also a must. They help separate valuable insights from background noise, allowing businesses to make informed decisions based on real-time data. If customer preferences shift suddenly, companies equipped with strong analytics can pivot their strategies without hesitation. Investing in the right tools isn't just beneficial—it's essential for staying ahead.

Competitive Analysis: Staying Sharp

A company that understands where it stands in relation to competitors is always better positioned for success. Competitive analysis helps in finding ways to differentiate and capitalize on emerging opportunities. Whether it's refining pricing models, improving service quality, or adopting new technologies, a strong grasp of the competitive landscape helps businesses stay one step ahead.

In a world where change is constant, adaptability is a fundamental part of staying relevant. Businesses that embrace market research, flexible strategies, and continuous feedback loops position themselves for long-term success. Staying agile ensures that when the market shifts, your business moves with it—not after it.

Developing a Culture of Learning and Growth

Today, businesses that encourage learning and growth are staying ahead. The idea of continuous improvement is what separates thriving organizations from those struggling to keep pace. When employees are constantly learning, they're more engaged, more innovative, and better equipped to meet evolving customer needs.

Making Learning an Everyday Practice

Think of an organization where learning is part of the daily routine. That's what continuous learning programs should aim for. These programs don't have to be rigid or overwhelming; they should invite curiosity, spark new ideas, and keep service strategies fresh. When employees actively engage with new information, they become more adaptable, ensuring the company remains competitive, no matter how quickly industries shift (*Continuous Learning Culture Defined*, 2025).

Encouraging Self-Assessment and Personal Growth

One of the most effective ways to foster growth is by giving employees the tools to assess their own progress. Encouraging self-assessment is more than pointing out weaknesses; it's helping individuals take ownership of their development. When employees regularly evaluate their own skills and contributions, they're more likely to take initiative and collaborate with colleagues to drive improvement.

For example, I once worked for a utility company for six months. I gave it my all—greeting coworkers with a cheery attitude every morning, dedicating time to learn the ins and outs of the company, and striving to provide excellent service. However, I soon realized that the customers were often hostile and aggressive. If they didn't pay their utility bill on time, we would shut off their utilities after 10 days.

In my 20 years of customer service, I had never been cursed at, threatened, or even belittled—until this job. It was the worst experience of my career. Despite my best efforts to remain professional and patient, the constant abuse became unbearable. I eventually left the company, giving a two-week notice, and decided that environment wasn't for me.

This experience taught me the importance of self-assessment and recognizing when a situation is beyond what I can handle. It also highlighted the incredible patience and resilience required in customer service roles. Not everyone understands the emotional toll that comes with dealing with difficult customers, but it's a reality many service professionals face daily.

Peer reviews and feedback sessions can transform self-assessment from an individual task into a shared experience, creating a culture where everyone is invested in success. Studies show that organizations that prioritize self-evaluation see higher engagement and stronger teamwork because employees feel accountable for their own and each other's progress (Verkooijen et al., 2024).

Providing the Right Resources for Growth

A strong learning culture is both about motivation and access. Companies need to make it easy for employees to find and use educational resources, whether that's through industry publications, online courses, or in-house training programs. Learning should fit seamlessly into employees' schedules, whether they're listening to a podcast on emerging trends during their commute or watching a short webinar over lunch. When learning is accessible and flexible, it stops feeling like a chore and becomes a natural part of daily work life.

Tracking Progress and Celebrating Growth

To keep momentum going, businesses need to measure and recognize progress. Metrics like customer satisfaction scores, efficiency improvements, and innovation rates provide clear evidence of how continuous learning benefits the organization. But numbers aren't the only way to track growth—employee and customer testimonials can be just as powerful. When employees see how their development positively impacts customers and the business, it reinforces their motivation to keep learning. Recognizing achievements, whether through public acknowledgment or small rewards, strengthens a culture where progress is valued and celebrated.

Guideline

1. **Set clear goals:** Align learning objectives with business success.
2. **Provide relevant training:** Focus on industry needs and future trends.
3. **Encourage self-assessment:** Use simple evaluation tools for growth.
4. **Ensure easy access:** Offer a knowledge hub or digital library.
5. **Track progress:** Measure impact with metrics and feedback.

When businesses prioritize learning and development, they improve their services and build teams that are more engaged, adaptable, and motivated to excel. And that's the real key to long-term success.

Conclusion

Throughout this chapter, we've talked about why a mindset of continuous improvement is a game-changer for customer service. The secret is constantly finding ways to do better, serve smarter, and create stronger connections with customers. Feedback loops play a massive role in this process; they're a tool for real change. When businesses take customer insights seriously and act on them, they see the payoff in higher satisfaction, stronger loyalty, and even happier employees. After all, when teams see that their efforts are making a difference, engagement and morale skyrocket.

But it doesn't stop there. The real key to long-term success is staying adaptable. Markets shift, customer expectations evolve, and businesses that don't keep up get left behind. That's why regularly checking in with feedback is essential. It keeps teams accountable, ensures businesses stay relevant, and fosters a culture where improvement is always in motion. When continuous learning becomes second nature, everyone—from frontline employees to leadership—plays a part in making service better.

It all comes down to building stronger relationships—with customers, with teams, and within the organization itself. By embracing a culture of ongoing improvement, businesses set themselves up not just to survive but to thrive, delivering a standout service that keeps people coming back. The companies that make feedback, adaptation, and innovation a priority aren't just reacting to change—they're leading it.

Conclusion

Throughout this book, we've explored the many ways businesses can create outstanding customer experiences. At the core of it all is a simple truth: exceptional customer service is the foundation of business success. Companies that genuinely put customers first don't just see higher satisfaction and retention rates; they build reputations that fuel long-term growth. When customers feel valued, they stick around, tell their friends, and become loyal advocates. It's a win-win.

The Importance of Customer-Centric Practices

Focusing on the customer is a mindset that needs to be woven into every interaction, policy, and decision. Businesses that adopt customer-centric practices create stronger relationships, increase trust, and ultimately drive success. It's not about reacting to customer needs; it's about anticipating them and consistently delivering value.

Take the companies that have built their brands around customer obsession. They exceed expectations time and time again. Prioritizing customer experience improves retention and creates loyal fans who fuel growth through word-of-mouth and repeat business. When customer-centricity becomes the heartbeat of an organization, everything else falls into place.

The Role of Emotional Intelligence

One of the biggest revolutions in customer service is emotional intelligence. It's not just about solving problems; it's about how those problems are solved. A service rep who listens with empathy, responds with patience, and understands a customer's frustration resolves an issue, creating a positive experience that sticks with the customer long after the interaction is over.

Think about the last time you had an issue with a product or service. If the person helping you was dismissive or robotic, it probably left a bad taste in your mouth. But if they showed genuine concern and worked with you to find a solution, you likely walked away feeling valued. That's the power of emotional intelligence in action. Businesses that train their teams to recognize and manage emotions—both their own and their customers'—set themselves apart in a crowded market.

Practical Strategies for Implementation

Having the right mindset is one thing, but without clear strategies, it's easy for customer service goals to fall flat. That's why structured frameworks matter. They help teams stay consistent, responsive, and aligned with the company's overall vision for service excellence.

Simple strategies like active listening training, real-time feedback loops, and service blueprints can make all the difference. When employees have a clear roadmap to follow, they can focus on delivering great experiences without second-guessing how to handle situations. And when companies empower their teams with the right tools and support, service quality naturally improves. The key is to provide structure while still allowing flexibility—because no two customer interactions are ever exactly the same.

Commitment to Continuous Improvement

Customer expectations evolve constantly. What works today might not work tomorrow, which is why the best businesses never get too comfortable. They listen, adapt, and refine their strategies based on real customer feedback.

Continuous improvement means staying ahead of problems. Organizations that embrace change and actively seek out ways to do better are the ones that thrive. Whether it's through regular customer surveys, employee feedback sessions, or service innovation initiatives, the businesses that commit to ongoing growth are the ones that stand the test of time.

Final Thoughts

Great customer service isn't just about policies or processes—it's about people. It's about making real, human connections that leave a lasting impact. The businesses that truly thrive are the ones that stay customer-focused, emotionally intelligent, and always open to learning and evolving.

By embracing these principles, you're doing more than just improving service—you're creating experiences that matter. You're building relationships, strengthening trust, and fostering a culture where both employees and customers feel seen, heard, and valued. And that's what turns a good business into a great one. Here's to redefining what exceptional service looks like and inspiring others to do the same.

References

ArenaCX. (2023, December). *Personalization vs. efficiency: Striking the right balance in customer service.* ArenaCX. https://arenacx.com/personalization-vs-efficiency-striking-the-right-balance-in-customer-service/

Aventis Learning Group. (2021, May 19). *5 types of difficult customers (and how to handle them effectively).* Aventis Learning Group. https://aventislearning.com/5-types-of-difficult-customers-and-how-to-handle-them-effectively/

Bennett, A. (2024). *Handling 5 types of difficult customers effectively.* Business Innovation Facility. https://businessinnovationfacility.org/5-types-difficult-customers-help/

Blair, A. (2025, January 21). *Why emotion is the most important customer experience metric.* Retail TouchPoints. https://www.retailtouchpoints.com/features/executive-viewpoints/why-emotion-is-the-most-important-customer-experience-metric

Blog - Semos Cloud. (2024, December 26). *Semos Cloud.* https://semoscloud.com/resources/blog/

Borowski, C. (2024, April). *Emotional intelligence in customer service: The secret ingredient to satisfied, loyal customers.* The CX Lead.

https://thecxlead.com/insights/emotional-intelligence-customer-service/

Brereton, J. (2024, May 6). The power of the product feedback loop: Enhancing customer satisfaction. *LaunchNotes.* https://www.launchnotes.com/blog/the-power-of-the-product-feedback-loop-enhancing-customer-satisfaction

Brett, C. (2024, September 16). *I*ntegrating feedback loops to enhance service quality in customer-facing teams. *Analytics 365.* https://www.analytics-365.com/blog/integrating-feedback-loops-to-enhance-service-quality/

Bridges, M. (2024, April 8). *Top 10 customer-centric design (CCD) frameworks used by consultants.* Medium. https://mark-bridges.medium.com/top-10-customer-centric-design-ccd-frameworks-used-by-consultants-fd948886d259

Building a customer experience vision. (n.d.). Qualtrics. https://www.qualtrics.com/experience-management/customer/building-a-customer-experience-vision/

Call Center Studio. (2023, April 22). *The importance of empathy in customer service.* Call Center Studio. https://callcenterstudio.com/contact-center-best-practices/the-importance-of-empathy-in-customer-service/

Cerdeira, C. (2018, February 22). 12 conflict resolution tips for excellent customer service. *Talkdesk.* https://www.talkdesk.com/blog/12-conflict-resolution-tips-for-excellent-customer-service/

Communication barriers in customer service. (2024, July 10). Barriers To Communication. https://barrierstocommunication.com/communication-barriers-in-customer-service/

Continuous learning culture defined. (2025). Aurora Training Advantage. https://auroratrainingadvantage.com/human-resources/key-term/continuous-learning-culture/

Develop customer-centric vision and culture. (n.d.). *ServiceTarget.* https://www.servicetarget.com/blog/develop-customer-centric-vision-and-culture

Dr. Henike, T. (2025, January 20). 4 types of innovation culture: Best tools and habits to drive yours. *ITONICS.* https://www.itonics-innovation.com/blog/innovation-culture

Dwivedi, R., Lohmor Choudhary, S., Dixit, R., Sahiba, Z., & Naik, S. (2024). The customer loyalty vs. customer retention: The impact of customer relationship management on customer satisfaction. *Web Intelligence, 22*(3), 1–18. https://doi.org/10.3233/web-230098

Emerson, M. S. (2021, August 30). 8 ways you can improve your communication skills. *Professional Development | Harvard DCE.* https://professional.dce.harvard.edu/blog/8-ways-you-can-improve-your-communication-skills/

Execs In The Know. (2024, April). *Human in the loop: An intersection of people and technology*. Execs in the Know. https://execsintheknow.com/magazines/april-2024-issue/human-in-the-loop-an-intersection-of-people-and-technology/

Ferrie, P. (2024, November 29). *The powerful impact of IT support on customer satisfaction.* Euro Systems. https://euro-systems.co.uk/news/the-powerful-impact-of-it-support-on-customer-satisfaction/

Fontanella, C. (2022, April 18). 16 customer experience trends & stats that'll define the next year. *HubSpot Blog*. https://blog.hubspot.com/service/customer-experience-trends

Franz, A. (2024, October 3). *7 ways to boost customers' emotional connection and loyalty with your brand.* MarTech. https://martech.org/7-ways-to-boost-customers-emotional-connection-and-loyalty-with-your-brand/

Freshchat: Customer messaging, live chat & chatbots | Freshworks. (2025). Freshworks; Freshchat: Customer Messaging, Live Chat & Chatbots |

Freshworks. https://www.freshworks.com/live-chat-software/

The FullStory Team. (2024). How AI is transforming customer experience for businesses. *Fullstory.com.* https://www.fullstory.com/blog/ai-in-customer-experience/

Furjanic, R. (2024, October 8). *The year-round importance of employee recognition and engagement: Lessons from National Customer Service Week.* Abel Personnel. https://www.abelpersonnel.com/the-year-round-importance-of-employee-recognition-and-engagement-lessons-from-national-customer-service-week/

Gherca, I. (2024, October 18). Mastering customer feedback: Top 16 tools to explore in 2024. *Touchpoint.* https://www.touchpoint.com/blog/top-customer-feedback-tools/

Gjellebæk, C., Svensson, A., Bjørkquist, C., Fladeby, N., & Grundén, K. (2020). Management challenges for future digitalization of healthcare services. *Futures, 124*(2). https://doi.org/10.1016/j.futures.2020.102636

Gonçalves, L. (2024, May 8). Business model innovation guide for leaders. *Adapt Methodology.* https://adaptmethodology.com/blog/business-model-innovation

Gupta, D. (2023, January 27). Resilience training in the workplace (+examples, tips). *Whatfix Blog*. https://whatfix.com/blog/resilience-training/

Heath, C. (2019). *10 ways to deliver good customer service*. Help Scout. https://www.helpscout.com/blog/good-customer-service/

Holder, E. (n.d.). Communication skills: 10 tips for effective communication. *Blog.jostle.me*. https://blog.jostle.me/blog/communication-skills

Iheagwara, C. (2024, April 26). *22 examples of customer retention strategies that actually work*. Simpu. https://simpu.co/post/examples-of-customer-retention-strategies/

James, G. (2018, April 9). Transforming negative sentiment into customer loyalty. *Beyond the Arc*. https://beyondthearc.com/blog/2018/customer-experience/negative-customer-experience-loyalty

Klimuk, E. (2023, June 14). *Emotional scoring: The new frontier in customer experience*. Supportbench. https://www.supportbench.com/emotional-scoring-the-new-frontier-in-customer-experience/

Linker, E. (2024, December 26). Data-driven decision-making: Data as a competitive advantage. *Improvado*. https://improvado.io/blog/data-driven-decision-making

Luck, I. (2024, December 5). 6 customer experience management frameworks for 2022. *CustomerGauge*. https://customergauge.com/blog/customer-experience-management-framework

M, T. (2025, January 25). Customer service de-escalation techniques that save deals. *Magellan Solutions*. https://www.magellan-solutions.com/blog/customer-service-de-escalation-techniques-that-save-deals/

Magids, S. (2015, November). *The new science of customer emotions*. Harvard Business Review. https://hbr.org/2015/11/the-new-science-of-customer-emotions

Manly, J., Harnoss, J., Schmitt, H. L., Werner, R., Blanchard, D., & Lovich, D. (2023, July 24). *An innovation culture that gets results*. BCG Global. https://www.bcg.com/publications/2023/innovation-culture-strategy-that-gets-results

Marketing Evolution. (2020, July 22). *The importance of flexibility in marketing analytics*. Marketing Evolution. https://www.marketingevolution.com/knowledge-center/importance-of-flexibility-marketing-analytics

Martinuzzi, B. (2023, October 2). *Customer service skills: Using emotional intelligence to make a connection*. American Express Business Class.

https://www.americanexpress.com/en-us/business/trends-and-insights/articles/customer-service-skills-using-emotional-intelligence-to-make-a-connection/

Maximizing Customer Experience through Interdepartmental Collaboration | Guidde. (2023, May 22). *Guidde.* https://www.guidde.com/blog/maximizing-customer-experience-through-interdepartmental-collaboration

Nicastro, D. (2023, November 6). *A collaborative departmental approach to the customer experience model.* CMSWire. https://www.cmswire.com/customer-experience/how-cross-department-collaboration-fuels-a-customer-experience-model/

Noble Desktop. (2024, July 20). *Adapting to market trends: The role of flexibility in strategy.* Noble Desktop. https://www.nobledesktop.com/learn/digital-marketing/adapting-to-market-trends-the-role-of-flexibility-in-strategy

Park, S. G., & Park, K. H. (2018). Correlation between nonverbal communication and objective structured clinical examination score in medical students. *Korean Journal of Medical Education, 30*(3), 199–208. https://doi.org/10.3946/kjme.2018.94

Paryvai, M. (2024, February 5). 4 customer satisfaction metrics (NPS, CSAT, CES, & more). *Missive.* https://missiveapp.com/blog/customer-satisfaction-metrics

Perzynska, K. (2024). How to use emotions to improve customer experience. *Survicate.* https://survicate.com/blog/emotional-customer-experience/

Peterka, P. (2024, August 9). *COVID-19 situation: Six Sigma ongoing training announcements.* SixSigma.us. https://www.6sigma.us/process-improvement/process-improvement-plan/

Poletto, S. (2023, June 28). The power of emotional intelligence in customer relations. *EmailTree AI.* https://emailtree.ai/blog/customer-service-skills/the-power-of-emotional-intelligence-in-customer-relations/

Pollack, J. (2024, May 23). Active listening in customer service: Importance, skills & examples. *Peaceful Leaders Academy.* https://peacefulleadersacademy.com/blog/active-listening-customer-service/

The Power of Brand Milestones: Leveraging Your Brand's Special Events. (2023, July 18). *Quill Creative Studio.* https://www.quillcreativestudio.com/blog/the-power-of-brand-milestones-leveraging-your-brands-special-events

Pratt, M. (2024, July 24). *How to build lasting loyalty from negative customer experiences.* Kobie Marketing. https://kobie.com/how-to-build-lasting-loyalty-from-negative-customer-experiences/

Process Frameworks. (n.d.). APQC. https://www.apqc.org/process-frameworks

Raileanu, G. (2018, September 12). A guide to customer satisfaction metrics - NPS vs CSAT and CES. *Retently.* https://www.retently.com/blog/customer-satisfaction-metrics/

Reji, R. (2023, November 14). The 7 key elements of effective customer service. *Hiver.* https://hiverhq.com/blog/elements-of-customer-service

Riegger, A.-S., Merfeld, K., Klein, J. F., & Henkel, S. (2022). Technology-enabled personalization: Impact of smart technology choice on consumer shopping behavior. *Technological Forecasting and Social Change, 181*(121752). https://doi.org/10.1016/j.techfore.2022.121752

Roosa, A. (2024, March 6). A customer service guide to conflict resolution. *Zendesk.* https://www.zendesk.com/blog/customer-service-guide-conflict-resolution/

Sharma, S. (2025a, January 29). Emotion detection: Deriving sentiments from customer feedback. *Zonka Feedback.* https://www.zonkafeedback.com/blog/emotion-detection

Sharma, S. (2025b, January 31). Top 22 customer feedback tools you can use in 2024. *Zonka Feedback.* https://www.zonkafeedback.com/blog/customer-feedback-tools

Sourabh-Hajela. (2024, July 10). *Achieving IT-business alignment with the MIT strategic alignment model: A comprehensive guide.* CIO Portal. https://cioindex.com/reference/comprehensive-guide-mit-strategic-alignment-model/

Stobierski, T. (2019, August 26). The advantages of data-driven decision-making. *Harvard Business School Online.* https://online.hbs.edu/blog/post/data-driven-decision-making

Strategic Alignment - the Ultimate Guide. (2019). Transparent Choice. https://www.transparentchoice.com/strategic-alignment

Subhashis, J. (2024, February 12). 6 ways to deliver high-touch customer service. *Sprinklr.* https://www.sprinklr.com/blog/high-touch-customer-service/

Suley, W., & Yuanqiong, H. (2019). The impact of CSR reputation and customer loyalty. *International Journal of Research in Business and Social Science, 8*(4), 185–198. https://doi.org/10.20525/ijrbs.v8i4.302

Talebi, H., & Bardsiri, A. K. (2023, August). *The impact of information technology on service quality, satisfaction, and customer relationship management.* ResearchGate. https://www.researchgate.net/publication/372822768_The_Impact_of_Information_Technology_on_Service_Quality_Satisfaction_and_Customer_Relationship_Management_Case_Study_IT_Organization_Individuals

The Art of Resilience. (2024). *Berkeley Exec Ed.* https://executive.berkeley.edu/thought-leadership/blog/art-resilience

10 best customer service strategies for unmatched satisfaction. (2025). Nice. https://www.nice.com/info/mastering-unified-cx-across-channels-top-strategies-tools

Tousley, S. (2019). *Customer feedback strategy: The only guide you'll ever need.* HubSpot. https://www.hubspot.com/customer-feedback

Trinet. (2023, December 4). *Common challenges with employee training.* Trinet. https://www.trinet.com/insights/common-challenges-with-employee-training

University of Texas. (2020, November 3). *How much of communication is nonverbal?* The University of Texas Permian Basin. https://online.utpb.edu/about-us/articles/communication/how-much-of-communication-is-nonverbal/

VanBockel, T. (2024, December 21). *How CEOs can build agile business plans for evolving markets*. Attorney Aaron Hall. https://aaronhall.com/how-ceos-can-build-agile-business-plans-for-evolving-markets/

Verkooijen, M. H. M., van Tuijl, A. A. C., Calsbeek, H., Fluit, C. R. M. G., & van Gurp, P. J. (2024). How to evaluate lifelong learning skills of healthcare professionals: A systematic review on content and quality of instruments for measuring lifelong learning. *BMC Medical Education, 24*(1). https://doi.org/10.1186/s12909-024-06335-9

Waite, R. (2024, August 7). 6 call center de-escalation techniques for customer service. *Robin Waite*. https://www.robinwaite.com/blog/6-call-center-de-escalation-techniques-for-customer-service

Wellington, E. (2022, November 21). The 8 best ways to collect customer feedback. *Help Scout*. https://www.helpscout.com/blog/customer-feedback/

Wilson, M. (2023, July 4). The benefits of peer-to-peer recognition in the workplace. *Bucketlist*.

https://bucketlistrewards.com/blog/benefits-of-peer-to-peer-recognition/

Wintermantel, H. (2024, May 2). Customer expectations: How to meet rising demands. *Zendesk.* https://www.zendesk.com/blog/customer-expectations-meet-rising-demands/

Wong, K. (2023, August 12). 12 best practices for peer-to-peer recognition. *Engage Blog.* https://www.achievers.com/blog/peer-to-peer-recognition/

Zahidi, F., Kaluvilla, B. B., & Mulla, T. (2024). Embracing the new era: Artificial intelligence and its multifaceted impact on the hospitality industry. *Journal of Open Innovation: Technology, Market, and Complexity, 10*(4), 100390. https://doi.org/10.1016/j.joitmc.2024.100390

Zay, L. (2024, March 22). Key strategies to overcome communication barriers and communicate effectively. *HiHello Blog.* https://www.hihello.com/blog/strategies-to-overcome-communication-barriers-and-communicate-effectively/

Made in the USA
Columbia, SC
15 March 2025